D0955576

Moving Up to Millions

THE LIFE CALCULATOR GUIDE TO WEALTH

Kathleen Connell

John Wiley & Sons, Inc.

Copyright © 2007 by Kathleen Connell. All rights reserved.

Published by John Wiley & Sons, Inc., Hoboken, New Jersey.
Published simultaneously in Canada.

Wiley Bicentennial Logo: Richard J. Pacifico

No part of this publication may be reproduced, stored in a retrieval system, or
transmitted in any form or by any means, electronic, mechanical, photocopying,
recording, scanning, or otherwise, except as permitted under Section 107 or 108 of
the 1976 United States Copyright Act, without either the prior written permission
of the Publisher, or authorization through payment of the appropriate per-copy fee
to the Copyright Clearance Center, Inc., 222 Rosewood Drive, Danvers, MA 01923,
(978) 750-8400, fax (978) 646-8600, or on the Web at www.copyright.com. Requests
to the Publisher for permission should be addressed to the Permissions Department,
John Wiley & Sons, Inc., 111 River Street, Hoboken, NJ 07030, (201) 748-6011,
fax (201) 748-6008, or online at http://www.wiley.com/go/permissions.

Limit of Liability/Disclaimer of Warranty: While the publisher and author have
used their best efforts in preparing this book, they make no representations
or warranties with respect to the accuracy or completeness of the contents of
this book and specifically disclaim any implied warranties of merchantability
or fitness for a particular purpose. No warranty may be created or extended
by sales representatives or written sales materials. The advice and strategies
contained herein may not be suitable for your situation. You should consult with
a professional where appropriate. Neither the publisher nor author shall be liable
for any loss of profit or any other commercial damages, including but not limited
to special, incidental, consequential, or other damages.

For general information on our other products and services or for technical
support, please contact our Customer Care Department within the United States at
(800) 762-2974, outside the United States at (317) 572-3993 or fax (317) 572-4002.

Wiley also publishes its books in a variety of electronic formats. Some content that
appears in print may not be available in electronic formats. For more information
about Wiley products, visit our Web site at www.wiley.com.

Library of Congress Cataloging-in-Publication Data
  Connell, Kathleen M.
    Moving up to millions: the life calculator guide to wealth / Kathleen Connell.
      p. cm.
    Includes bibliographical references.
    ISBN 978-0-470-13181-7 (cloth)
    1. Finance, Personal. I. Title.
    HG179.C66463 2007
    332.024'01–dc22   2007004997

Printed in the United States of America
10 9 8 7 6 5 4 3 2 1

To my sons, Adam and Garrett,
who are worth more than millions to me

To my mother and late father,
both of whom served as my financial mentors

Contents

Introduction

Journey to Millionaire Status

In researching this book, I spoke to hundreds of Americans across the country who, regardless of their income, education, geographic location, or family profile, share a common dream of financial security—a goal that will enable them to be economically independent and capable of caring for themselves and their families, despite any personal or economic setbacks. However, they recognize that they often lack the knowledge needed to effectively plan their life journey and reduce the risks associated with events beyond their control. It is in response to these concerns that I have written this book, to offer the education, strategies, and tools needed to empower each of them, and you, as you seek to attain your own financial goals.

Despite our hopes for a comfortable life, many in America have a tremendous fear of economic uncertainty—the premonition that our future will not be as secure as that of our parents; a strong belief that the next generations will be more at risk; a recognition that our resources will rapidly dissolve if we are faced with adverse life events; and a growing dismay that neither our employers, nor federal or state governments, will respond with the policies needed to protect us from economic duress.

Although those with college and graduate educations in white-collar jobs *appear* to be economically secure, many are articulate about their growing financial anxiety. In some cases, they are angry that, despite their hard work and focused efforts, their retirement, healthcare, and continued employment in a high-status career are very much threatened. Often saddled with super-sized mortgages on expensive homes, tuition bills for private schools, and high-premium insurance policies, they now face the responsibilities of caring for their aging parents and feel vulnerable to costly illnesses, disability, and inadequate retirement plans.

For Americans who lack both high wages and solid educational backgrounds, their futures seem particularly uncertain. Any of a dozen adverse events discussed in this book could easily disrupt their chances of a secure retirement. They worry about their ability to pay for family healthcare, to assume responsibility for the care of an extended family, or even to finance their children's education in public universities. Faced with multiple adverse events, the probabilities of which are defined in this book, their financial security will be jeopardized and their future opportunities dramatically altered.

We, as Americans, whether in professional and executive positions, blue-collar jobs, or salaried middle-class careers, know we are working harder and longer with fewer benefits and, importantly, we know that we face uncertain future prospects. Despite historic increases in home appreciation and increasing ownership of equities, many of the vast middle class are concerned that they are not sharing the benefits of the current period of economic growth. They are increasingly troubled by the specter of potential job loss and a lower standard of living due to continued globalization.

Regardless of any well-intentioned efforts at the congressional level to address the issues affecting middle-class Americans— healthcare, Medicare, retirement, job creation, and education—it will be many years before such policies, if enacted, are implemented. Waiting for the passage of magic-bullet legislation that may assist in mitigating, at some future point, the looming financial challenges is an ill-advised strategy that will only serve to delay progress toward a more solid economic foundation. It is crucial that each individual and family personally initiate actions to create its own framework for economic independence and security.

A multitude of books are available for individuals to equip themselves to create winning investment strategies, to review shortfalls in savings, to reduce debt, to manage their taxes and estates, and to create retirement lifestyles on sandy beaches or lush golf courses.

High-net-worth individuals may even employ expensive financial advisors who will set well-defined asset allocation strategies.

Focusing solely on investment returns, however, is an incomplete and shortsighted approach to achieving financial success. It will result in a failure to be prepared for life events that can, overnight, turn positive investment returns into negative cash flow. Investment strategies are not sufficient by themselves to achieve financial goals. Although high returns may be achieved on an investment portfolio, failure to mitigate risks that occur over your lifetime will offset any investment gains.

It is changing life events—divorce, sudden family expenses, uncovered healthcare costs, major disability, investment losses, unexpected inheritance, and a second career, to name only a few—that dramatically affect financial security. These cannot generally be anticipated. It is the ability to predict risks and to offset it with pragmatic action strategies that makes the Life Calculator so valuable.

The distinctive tools of the software program Life Calculator and its associated Web site, www.LifeCalculator.Net, offer you the opportunity to create unlimited alternative strategies to achieve financial security. Using the powerful Life Calculator, you will set your own financial goals and create an individualized financial plan that assures your economic security. The dynamic and interactive tool of the Life Calculator will test alternative strategies to achieve your objectives, responding to any changes in your life circumstances that may alter the availability of financial resources or impose significant unexpected costs.

The Life Calculator is the *only* financial engine that incorporates both investment advice and personal what-if scenario simulations on life events. It provides its readers with the sophisticated financial advice of a highly paid private banker, while adding the power of calculating the impact of any myriad of future life scenarios on your retirement savings, potential second career plans, and investment opportunities.

Using the Life Calculator, you are able to assume responsibility as your own financial advisor. After you complete your personal financial plan and test the impact of potential adverse life events, you will be armed with printouts of your financial results. This information will allow you to discuss objectively with your spouse, employer, accountant, and investment advisor alternative financial goals and strategies that are most appropriate for a particular life-cycle period.

Contrast your life with the two dozen profiles of individuals and families presented in the book and software program and the proven strategies they use to achieve millionaire or multimillionaire status. Whether working in construction, nursing, teaching, government, technology, advertising, or real estate, these individuals embody the four rules of making millions: *Own Your Future, Reduce Risk, Make Time Your Ally,* and *Master Change.*

Moving Up to Millions also provides 20 easy-to-complete exercises covering often-encountered decisions in life. Are you advantaged in buying a large home or a small home and investing the difference? What is your financial breakeven measure for the purchase of long-term care insurance? How many more years should you work, and how much more savings will you need, if you assume you live to age 90? 95? Target and value a second career—how much can you earn? What is the best time to sell your home? The *Life Calculator* shows the impact that these typical life-cycle decisions, and many others, have on the reader's personal balance sheet.

Using the Life Calculator, you can be proactive in taking charge of your financial future. Whether you have limited savings in the bank when you begin reading this book or have accumulated millions in investments, the same rules apply. Whether you are beginning your financial journey in your early 20s or are still struggling in your 60s to attain sufficient economic resources, you will find this book valuable.

Contrary to some authors, who hype the outdated myth that there is a *number,* the target savings needed to support your family in a comfortable retirement, this book recognizes the multidimensional nature of life's experiences. *Moving Up to Millions* presents a sophisticated analysis of life's multiple adverse events and positive life-changing opportunities that may dramatically affect your financial security. This Rubix Cube approach of integrating various financial scenarios confirms the need for a sophisticated strategy that identifies a range of potential numbers.

To be successful in charting a secure economic course, you cannot be passive and reactive. You must constantly focus on becoming prosperous, defined as having sufficient financial resources to live *your* ideal life, believing that you can take the actions necessary to create a financially secure future. You must identify your goals, seek the advice of those who can further educate you regarding appropriate financial decisions, and remain open to new life strategies.

As you journey toward your personal goals and achieve important milestones in your life, take the opportunity to celebrate. Relish your victories and share important times with family and friends. Although financial security is an important goal, the journey is as important as the destination. Do not press yourself to constantly move forward to grab the next promotion, purchase the bigger home, acquire the more expensive car, or send your children to prestigious colleges, all the while saying to yourself "When this is completed, I will then be happy."

Cherish each day, be thankful for each opportunity, express gratitude to those who support you, and leave a legacy each step of the way. Count your daily blessings, recognize your progress toward your financial goals, and share your new confidence and financial power with others. These daily expressions will have a more lasting effect than any estate you could bequeath at the completion of your life journey.

The Life Calculator™ Online Program

Welcome to your complimentary 30-day membership in the LifeCalculator.Net online community! To begin using the Life Calculator™, you will need an internet connection to access www.LifeCalculator.Net. At the login screen, you will be presented with three different login options. You can login as a Visitor, Guest, or Member. As a purchaser of this book, you are entitled to a free 30-day limited Guest access to the website.

After clicking on the Guest login, you will be asked to create a login name and to fill in some contact details. The Web site will also ask you to find a code word in this book. Once you have filled in the correct code word, your account will be created and you will receive an e-mail with a temporary password. In future visits to LifeCalculator.Net, you will be able to directly log onto the Web site.

Your account is valid for 30 days.* At any time during the 30 days, you have the opportunity to activate a full membership at a discounted price, joining the Life Calculator™ community and expanding your access to the complete power of the Life Calculator™ technology, its frequent expert panels, extensive databases, and valuable current investment information.

I am excited to have this opportunity to share the powerful Life Calculator™ platform with you and look forward to meeting you online!

KATHLEEN CONNELL, PH.D.

---

*This offer is valid through May 31, 2008 or until the Web site, LifeCalculator.Net is no longer operational, whichever comes first.

Acknowledgments

This book marks a personal journey that has been a remarkable experience. In researching the challenges facing ordinary Americans in securing their financial futures, I have been inspired by the personal stories and grateful to the dozens of people who were willing to share their financial hopes and concerns. They have encouraged me to shift my initial writing from an academic discussion of the crisis of baby boomer retirements to a positive, pragmatic set of strategies—complete with state-of-the-art computer technology support—that will empower them to be financially independent, despite life's challenges. It is their stories that are the basis for the two dozen hypothetical profiles which guide the financial engine of the Life Calculator, the book's online software component.

As a first-time author, I have been most fortunate in having been introduced to the "A" team of the publishing world. Richard Pine, my brilliant book agent, took on an unpublished author and was a tireless advocate for my multimedia project. A very special thanks to Peter Barnes, who was a great cheerleader and a wonderful resource, tutoring me in the publishing industry and providing countless references for others who became my circle of support. My writing benefited from the skilled editing of Jim Wade, who also contributed greatly in educating me to the nuances of the book world. Elaine English, Laura Smith, and Milton Springut have proven to be smart, savvy legal eagles who have protected me from costly errors.

The entire team at John Wiley has been a source of encouragement, enthusiasm and sage advice. I was gifted with Debra Englander as my executive editor. Convinced that my book had a unique contribution to readers, she assembled a highly talented group to support my efforts. A deep sense of gratitude to Stacey Fischkelta, Senior Production Editor, for her gifted editing and efforts to refine my prose; to Charles Vagnone for his skilled copyediting; to Michelle Fitzgerald, Bonnie Reddington, and PJ Campbell for their marketing expertise; to Michael Freeland for his visionary book design; and to Greg Friedman and Stacey Small whose organizational efforts made a difference.

Among my literary circle of friends, my personal appreciation to Arianna Huffington, Larry Elder, Peter Navarro, and Ted Fishman, who offered their support and relationships to further my book efforts. I am truly in debt to those friends who shared generously of their time to read the manuscript, review design concepts, suggest media strategies, and provide invaluable advice and comments: Karen Baynard, Greg Clow, Tula Connell, Trish Donnelly, Susan Kennedy, Betty Hudson, Catherine Malloy, Jill Schuker, Karen Stephanson, and Marla Wolfe. A huge hug for my friends—and especially the Women's Poker Club—for their encouragement, excitement, and unceasing support.

My research efforts were supported by Nancy Bolton, Catherine Lewis, and the confidence of my fellow faculty and staff at the Haas Graduate School of Business at UC Berkeley, who were convinced of my ability to create an "online" financial advisor for those seeking to "move up to millions." I am truly indebted to Enoch Cheng, my research assistant, whose talent, tireless hard work, and incredible loyalty have brought this book project to completion and achieve the vision of a Web-based financial planning resource.

For those in my professional circle of friends, Dean Al Osborne, Dean Tom Campbell, Dennis Tito, and Jack Ehnes—my deepest thanks for your thoughtful advice, experienced critique and strong endorsement. To Andy Stern and SEIU, the management of the National Education Association, and California Teachers Association—my gratitude for "road testing" the program and verifying its usefulness.

On a personal note, my deep gratitude to Jeremy Carper, whose positive attitude and deep belief that this book offered value to others gave me the confidence to continue, even when encountering obstacles. Without the support of my families—the Connells, Asays, and Almys—I would never have had the courage to begin.

My teenage sons have been the real heroes—so very understanding and patient during extended months of research and writing. I am so very proud of them, thankful for their love and support, and dedicate this book to them.

CHAPTER 1

Meet Your Neighbors

M*oving Up to Millions* offers you a multidimensional opportunity to create financial strategies that are unique to your own circumstances. In moving toward a goal of financial independence and millionaire wealth, you will have the opportunity to call on multiple resources. You will learn by completing financial exercises; reading the profiles of individuals and families—from union workers to top executives—who have met the challenges of becoming millionaires; drawing on the resources of hyperlinks and Web-based informational sources to gain knowledge; and making your own financial plan using the Life Calculator. You will become an active participant on your journey to multimillionaire status.

Life profiles of Americans are re-created throughout this book by 10 hypothetical families and individuals whose experiences may mirror your own or that of your neighbors. (On the Life Calculator Web site, www.LifeCalculator.Net, additional profiles are available, enabling you to identify with those individuals or families facing challenges similar to your own.) In reading the financial challenges they face and their responses to life events, you will be educated to various financial strategies that you can employ in your own life to mitigate negative events and to maximize opportunities. You will be encouraged to engage in appropriate financial responses to advance your own personal agenda.

1

Figure 1.1   Life Calculator Profiles

Profiles are described for people who are in their 40s up to people in their 70s. Figure 1.1 shows the 10 Life Calculator profiles that represent a range of incomes from $42,000 to $225,000, with career fields as varied as nursing, clinical research, hospitality services, teaching, construction, law enforcement, advertising, law, bioscience, real-estate, and technology.

These Life Calculator profiles, seven couples and three individuals, have encountered personal challenges ranging from divorce, disability, loss of jobs, volatile income, unreimbursed healthcare costs, unfunded pensions, caregiving of parents, and investment losses. In response, they have proven resilient by identifying successful second careers, taking care of aging families in their own home, restructuring investment portfolios following major losses, recovering from serious injury, finding cost-saving methods of financing college, and regaining financial stability following costly divorces.

Life Calculator Profiles

Vivian Blackboard—Denver, Colorado. Age 40, divorced, income of $89,000.

Vivian was recently promoted to the position of executive director of a nonprofit healthcare organization. She is in the process of adopting a child and purchasing a home.

Challenges: She has past poor credit due to excessive consumer debt remaining from marriage, a lack of a pension, and final payments on a mid-career MBA loan.

Marla and Bill Newton—Atlanta, Georgia. Ages 46 and 48, 10-year-old twins. Marla earns $55,000 and Bill earns $115,000, including a bonus.

Marla and Bill were entrepreneurs with uncertain cash flows that made them rethink their careers. They left their entrepreneurial positions to become a high school guidance counselor and coach and a real-estate manager.

Challenges: They have volatile income, lack of a pension, childcare expenses, aging parents, and uninsured healthcare/therapy costs for child injured in ski accident.

James and Nancy Razor—Greensboro, North Carolina. Ages 43 and 40, two children, ages 6 and 2. James earns $62,000 and Nancy earns $75,000.

James is a policeman; Nancy is a public attorney. Their income growth is limited, but they have strong retirement security.

Challenges: Cash-flow pressure, care of an aging parent, and college expenses for their children are all concerns.

Dan and Christina Apple—New York, New York. Ages 53 and 35. Dan earns $225,000. (Christina earns a beginning salary of $42,000 a year after completing her college education.) Dan has two teenagers from his first marriage; Christina just had a baby.

He is a marketing professional rebuilding his personal finances after poor life decisions.

Challenges: Dan is recently divorced, has expensive child support obligations, and has suffered serious investment losses. Dan and Christina are a new family with a baby.

Eric Router—Portland, Oregon. Age 50, single, earning $100,000. Eric is an outdoor enthusiast, active in the local art community, who values the flexibility of his freelance real estate appraisal role.

Challenges: Real estate investment losses, litigation costs with tenants, and no health insurance have cautioned Eric to be more conservative in his finances.

Jack and Cindy Palm—San Mateo, California. Ages 56 and 49, with three teenagers. Jack, a computer technology executive, lost his $250,000 salaried job due to offshoring of his position to India. After extended unemployment and only temporary consulting jobs, he accepted a permanent job at $160,000.

The Palms have an expensive lifestyle to maintain, with private schools and club memberships.

Challenges: The Palms must adjust to three years of un-employment, career reeducation expenses, downsizing family budget by $90,000 to fit new salary, and financing college for three children.

Adriana Dell—Orlando, Florida. Age 61, son in early 20s, earning $60,000.

Adriana is a divorced single parent. She is an emergency room nurse with good benefits and a secure retirement.

Challenges: Divorced at age 51, she had a low savings rate, no pension, and a limited investment portfolio.

Ken and Mary Blackberry—Houston, Texas. Ages 60 and 54, Both had prior marriages and now have a blended family of four children, two still in college. Ken and Mary are displaced Enron professionals who relocated to secure employment. Ken earns $95,000 and Mary earns $104,000 in their second careers.

Challenges: Double job losses in their 50s and loss of pensions re-quire the Blackberrys to start over in saving for retirement. They need to contribute to their children's college education.

Hank and Trudy Trio—Peoria, Illinois. Ages 76 and 71, with 5 children, 17 grandchildren. Prior to retirement, Hank earned $75,000 and Trudy earned $47,000.

The Trios just moved to Las Vegas, Nevada. They were in the construction and hospitality industries.

Challenges: Reality of caring for three aging parents, rebuilding retirement accounts drained by healthcare expenses, and delayed retirement. Worked an additional five years.

Peter and Betty Moto—Minneapolis, Minnesota. Ages 76 and 75, with four children. Peter had $200,000 income prior to retirement. They recently moved to Sedona, Arizona.

He is a bioengineer with stock options; prior employment as college professor.

Challenges: Three years of hospital and rehabilitation expenses for uninsured, injured son has depleted retirement savings; they have a trust fund for second son, who has autism.

Moving Up to Millions

The families in the 10 profiles examined work hard to achieve their personal dreams. Each family encounters setbacks that challenge its ability to reach goals; and each adopts new strategies to regain financial security. Whether they work in blue-collar jobs, own their own businesses, or serve in high-professional positions, all of the people who are profiled hope to become millionaires or multimillionaires. If they have already achieved the status of a seven-figure net worth, their goal will be to maintain that status and seek opportunities to further expand their financial assets.

A millionaire is defined as someone whose total net worth exceeds the seven-figure range, including all financial assets: their personal residence; all investments; the value of all defined benefits, 401(k)s, and other retirement assets; and all savings. Millionaire status is based on the projected appreciation value of an individual or couple's assets with a total net worth value determined at the time of their expected retirement. Appreciation factors related to each asset category are available for your review in the profiles section in Chapters 8 and 9.

You, Too, Can Be a Millionaire!

What financial factors must be present to enable an individual earning $60,000 a year, or a family earning $122,000, to become millionaires? Is that really a possibility? Yes, as Adriana Dell, a nurse; Vivian Blackboard, a nonprofit executive; Hank and Trudy Trio, union workers; and Bill and Marla Newton, a high school guidance counselor and real-estate executive, confirm! All of them have assets over a million dollars at the time of their retirement.

If multimillionaire status is your goal, what factors beyond income assure you of reaching that status? As you read through this book, you will be given specific tips on investments, second careers, protecting against financial loss, benefit-rich jobs, and maximizing the value of your home investment, which will guide you on your financial journey to multimillionaire status. James and Nancy Razor, a police officer and a public attorney; Eric Router, a real-estate appraiser; Dan and Christina Apple, an advertising executive and a lab technician, all have achieved multimillionaire status, with assets valued between $2 million and $3 million.

Achieving a higher level of financial wealth, having accumulated over $3 million in riches, are Peter and Betty Moto, a bioscience executive and an arts enthusiast; Jack and Cindy Palm, a technology manager and stay-at-home mother; and Mary and Ken Blackberry, a CPA and an adjunct professor/consultant. The Motos and the Palms both benefited from generous stock options, while the Blackberrys leveraged the sale of an expensive home and a downsized lifestyle to regain financial success following their double job/pension losses at Enron.

How do you make a million dollars? Many of you may have already experienced the triumph of a seven-figure bottom line, and some of you are eager to seek the status of a $3 million net worth or beyond. Having read the diverse strategies adopted by the hypothetical households, both individuals and couples, you may be surprised that they, like yourself, are still evaluating financial strategies and seeking additional financial knowledge. Their use of the tools in the Life Calculator improves their financial sophistication, preparing them to make the best decisions leading to greater financial security and increased wealth.

Their achievement of a million-dollar or multimillion-dollar status is not the gift of a trust fund or a parent. That is a legitimate avenue for personal wealth, but it occurs for a select number of Americans. Only one in five Americans age 43 to 61 receives an inheritance, with a typical sum of $64,000.[1] It is not wise to assume, unless you are certain of a windfall, that any such gift of dollars will be a factor in your achieving millionaire or multimillionaire status.

Rather, the strategies for becoming a millionaire are simple:

- Earn significant income that, when invested, can catapult you to millionaire status.
- Grow a million dollars or more through a diversified investment plan over a 20- to 30-year period.
- Purchase a home(s) that enjoys the benefits of appreciation over a 30-year period.
- Work in a benefit-rich job that provides generous healthcare and pension support.
- Leverage employer-provided benefits, investing to the maximum limit for employer-matched savings.
- Adopt a sound risk-management strategy incorporating appropriate health, long-term care, disability, and life insurance policies.
- Educate members of your immediate family on the importance of appropriate age-related insurance, reducing the probability that their uninsured status will burden you with financial costs.
- Win a national or state lottery—just joking!

Realistically, millionaire or multimillionaire status is the result of sound financial practices (living within your means and developing realistic savings goals); careers typified by hard work and superior performance; investing in real estate; protecting against the downside of adverse events through risk management; and leveraging the power of time and its associated compounding effects in a diversified investment strategy. Time is indeed your greatest ally in the journey to millionaire status.

Later in this chapter, the *Four Rules of Making Millions* will expand the discussion of strategies, and an in-depth review of the power of the Life Calculator in future chapters will facilitate your financial education. You will learn to track your own financial growth.

Begin now by considering your own financial situation. Apply strategies of the profiled families to your own life circumstances. By completing the following Life Calculator exercise, you may begin the positive steps to millionaire status.

Life Calculator Exercise ONE: You, Too, Can Be a Millionaire!

Connect to www.LifeCalculator.Net to create the scenarios under which you, too, can be a millionaire!

Not All Millionaires Are Equal

Although all 10 profiled families included in this book have worked hard to achieve their financial security and also their millionaire status, there is a significant difference in their net worth, ranging from a low of the Trios, a nonprofessional couple with barely a $1 million estate, to a high of $4.7 million for a Silicon Valley–based tech executive and his family. These millionaires would all view themselves as middle class, though with significantly different status, lifestyle, and financial security. The millionaires' wealth falls into three groups.

Bronze-Medal Millionaires ($1 Million to $2 Million)

Those having $1 million to $2 million are typically known as the *Bronze-Medal Millionaires*. This group is composed of four families: one, a nurse; two, a CPA; three, a married couple with a school counselor and a mid-level corporate executive; four, a union household with a construction foreman and a hospitality worker.

The Trios are fortunate to both have defined-benefit plans together valued at roughly half a million dollars, which at net present value for their extended longevity, estimated at a minimum

Table 1.1   One-Million-Dollar Status: Bronze Medal Millionaire

Family	401(k) Savings	Present Value of Defined Benefits	Home Value	Total Net Worth
Blackboard	$418,000	X	$780,000[a]	$1.2 million
Trios	$122,110	$588,028[b]	$500,000	$1.2 million
Dell	$470,000	X	$602,000[c]	$1.1 million
Newtons	$760,000	$475,130[d]	$525,000	$1.8 million

Notes:

[a] Home appreciates over a period of 30 years.

[b] Net present value of $52,500 (Hank) for 15 years and $32,900 for 18 years (Trudy) discounted at 5 percent. The number of years is the difference from retirement age to age 85.

[c] $450,000 home value at age 60, appreciating 6 percent over 5 years.

[d] Net present value of $38,130 for 20 years discounted at 5 percent.

of 85 years, adds significantly to the increase in their net worth. Hank Trio used his construction skills to build a well-designed five-bedroom home, which he sold in the appreciating market. Without the value of the defined benefits and home, the Trios would have a much-reduced estate.

The Newtons, former entrepreneurs, intentionally redirected their careers to employment opportunities with secure income and generous benefits. Marla specifically chose her job as a public high school guidance counselor and coach, as its hours coincided with that of her children's school day, saving the Newtons over $30,000 annually in childcare expenses. Bill Newton's employer-matched savings program complemented his wife's defined-benefit plan, and both contributed importantly to their economic security.

The two single women profiled, Adriana Dell and Vivian Blackboard, achieved millionaire status due to the rapid appreciation of their home residences and the value of their employer-matched savings programs, which both were diligent in maximizing.

Table 1.1 presents a comparison of the four families.

Silver-Medal Millionaires ($2 Million to $3 Million)

Those households having a net worth of $2 million to $3 million, known as silver-medal millionaires, are increasingly frequent, given the excessive home appreciation cycle during the past decade. For most Americans at this net worth level, the personal residence represents 40 percent of their assets. Appreciation in many housing markets has created a cohort of households whose property values grant them automatic millionaire status.

For the Apples, more than half of their net worth was created from the value of their home. However, in order to enjoy the benefits of their home value, the Apples will have to consider a strategy that would result in the sale of their home and the purchase of a less-expensive downsized residence, freeing up assets that can be reallocated to a more diverse portfolio that reflects their personal preferences regarding risk and liquidity.

The Razors' promotion to silver-medal millionaire status was a direct result of their employer pension plans, which comprised a large percentage of their final retirement wealth. They were also able to retire at age 55 from their public-sector jobs, enabling them to begin second careers, receiving valuable income while still collecting their generous public-sector defined-benefit pensions.

Eric Router, a single professional man, credits his aggressive real estate investing activities for his significant wealth. Ironically, that investment style exposed Eric to a high level of risk in an investment arena characterized by cyclical returns. He reconsiders his willingness to continue on a path of high-risk behavior and reallocates his $500,000 investment portfolio to a diversified stock, bonds, and mutual fund portfolio, while still owning a few selected real estate assets. Router also recognizes that he has not had to pay the significant costs of raising children, saving himself the substantial expense of $300,000 to $500,000, the amount it would take to raise a middle-class child from birth through college graduation.*

Comparisons of the silver-medal millionaires are presented in Table 1.2.

---

*It requires $284,460 to raise a child in urban areas in the West. Private college tuition estimated at $160,000 to $180,000. The costs would be higher if child attended a private high school. MSN Money Staff, "The Basics: Raising your quarter-million dollar baby," MSN citing USDA study, Retrieved from: http://moneycentral.msn.com/content/CollegeandFamily/Raisekids/P37245.asp

Table 1.2   Two-Million-Dollar Status: Silver Medal Millionaires

Family	401(k) Savings	Investments	Present Value of Defined Benefits	Home Value[a]	Total Net Worth
Router	X	$1.7 million[a]	X	$520,000	$2.2 million
Razors	$1.1 million	X	$928,090[b]	$300,000	$2.3 million
Apples	$1.2 million	X	N/A[c]	$1.6 million	$2.8 million

Notes:
[a] $650,000 compounded at 6 percent for 15 years. He originally had $850,000, but lost approximately $200,000 due to adverse events.
[b] Net present value of $89,415 for 15 years discounted at 5 percent.
[c] No assets in this category.

Gold-Medal Millionaires ($3 Million+)

The three highest-ranked multimillionaires profiled in this book, those having $3 million and above, are identified as gold-medal millionaires. Ken and Mary Blackberry, Peter and Betty Moto, and Jack and Cindy Palm achieve the impressive rank of gold-medal millionaires through entirely different avenues of wealth appreciation.

The Blackberrys, fired from their management positions at Enron, were able to finance their mid-career job changes due to the $700,000 net proceeds from the sale of their expensive Houston home. They made an important tactical decision: they relocated to the less expensive city of Austin and chose to buy a smaller home, placing $500,000 of their $700,000 home profit in an investment account, which grew substantially, together with their employer-matched contributions from their second career jobs.

Peter and Betty Moto benefited from the generous stock options Peter received as a biotech executive. Those options, together with the $1.4 million net profit of their home,* helped compensate for the $500,000 medical costs they paid to support their son's multiyear recovery from a near-fatal car accident. Peter Moto's willingness to

---

*Net home profit in this context is the amount remaining after payment of capital gains taxes and all commissions and fees related to the sale of the home or property.

work beyond his early expected retirement provided additional income that enabled them to enjoy a comfortable, though delayed, retirement in Sedona, Arizona.

The Palms' route to gold-medal status was based on Jack Palm's employment in two pre-IPO Silicon Valley companies that netted him significant options when they both went public. The appreciation of those options served as the basis of his personal wealth.

Jack regrets that soon after his second company went public, he lost his well-compensated position, due to offshoring the functions

Table 1.3   Three-Million-Dollar Status: Gold Medal Millionaire

Family	401(k) Savings	Stock Options	Present Value of Defined Benefits	Home Value	Total Net Worth
Blackberrys	$1.6 million	X	$701,760[a]	$812,030	$3.1 million
Motos	$722,000	$700,000	$872,354[b]	$1.4 million	$3.7 million
Palms	$1.4 million	$500,000	X	$2.8 million	$4.7 million

Note:
[a] Net present value of $67,610 for 15 years discounted at 5 percent.
[b] Net present value of $70,000 for 20 years discounted at 5 percent.

Table 1.4   Summary of Salaries and Assets of Profiles

Name(s)	Salaries	Total Assets
Adriana Dell	$60,000	$1.1 million
Hank and Trudy Trio	$75,000/$47,000	$1.2 million
Vivian Blackboard	$89,000	$1.2 million
Bill and Marla Newton	$115,000/$55,000	$1.8 million
Silver-Medal Millionaires		
Eric Router	$100,000	$2.2 million
James and Nancy Razor	$62,000	$2.3 million
Dan and Cindy Apple	$225,000/$42,000	$2.8 million
Gold-Medal Millionaires		
Ken and Mary Blackberry	$95,000/$104,000	$3.1 million
Peter and Betty Moto	$200,000	$3.7 million
Jack and Cindy Palm	$160,000	$4.7 million

to India. Jack was unable to secure a similar position in the industry, despite his credentials and active career search spanning a period of three years. He suffered three years of unemployment before taking a job at a salary of $160,000, but with an employer-matched savings program. The Palms are on the road to recovery!

See Table 1.3 to review the Gold-Medal Millionaires. See Table 1.4 for a summary of all three classifications.

Do You Really Need a Million Dollars?

Absolutely! A million-dollar lifestyle in 2007 is not a portrayal of a life of greed and wanton excess. Rather, it affords an individual or couple a reasonable lifestyle where they are financially independent and empowered to achieve their life goals. Recognizing the responsibilities of the club-sandwich generation and extended longevity of most Americans, achieving a millionaire or multimillionaire status simply helps ensure that your retirement will be characterized by comfort and security.

Fill in the blanks in Table 1.5. How many of the items have the power to erode your financial security? Total the costs associated

Table 1.5 Budgeting Your Million Dollars: Sizing Up Your Personal Expenses

One-time Costs

Item	Sample Value	Your Value
Buying a second vacation home or moving up	$400,000–$2,000,000	
Net worth loss through divorce	$25,000–$250,000	
Healthcare costs not paid for by insurance (over 25-year period)	$200,000–$300,000 (low) $300,000–$400,000 (medium) $400,000–$500,000 (high)	
Disability	$50,000–$300,000	
Underfunded pension	$200,000–$300,000	

(continued)

Table 1.5 *Continued*

Item	Sample Value	Your Value
Emergency fund for family expenses	3 months' salary	
Extended longevity (living to 90)	$100,000–$200,000	
Extended longevity (living to 95)	$200,000–$300,000	
Supplemental financial support for "boomerang" children (children over 21 years of age returning home)	$5,000–$25,000	
Subtotal		
Postretirement Costs (Assume for a Period of 20 Years)		
Car purchase	$25,000–$60,000/ car (usually 3 to 6 cars over 20 years)	
Personal care of an aging parent in your home	$7,000/year × Number of years (identify years of caregiving support)	
Assisted-living residence for one person	$70,000–$80,000/year (Number of people × Number of years)	
Volatile investment losses[a]	$10,000–$20,000/year (Assume no more than 1, 2, or 3 years)	
Hyperinflation[b]	$1,500–$3,000/year (Assume 1, 2, or 3 years)	
Your Subtotal		
Total Up Your Costs		
One-time costs		
Annual postretirement costs		
Total		

Notes:
[a] 4 percent loss on a portfolio of $250,000–$500,000.
[b] 3 percent loss in purchasing power of $50,000–$100,000.

with your selection. Note the difference between one-time costs and ongoing expenses.

Do your potential expenses surprise you? Whether you are beginning your pursuit of $1 million status, have achieved a seven-figure net worth, or are strategizing to leverage your multimillionaire status to further wealth increases, you may not have anticipated how quickly your million dollars will be spent on these nonbudgeted items, many of which are not within your control.

Advanced planning can substantially reduce many of these costs. The advice in this book and its accompanying Life Calculator software could save readers as much as $250,000, if you are responsive to the information and take the necessary action to mitigate against potential costs. See Table 1.6.

Table 1.6   Typical Life Calculator Savings

Event	Amount	Savings Tool
Assisted living or nursing home care	$300,000	Long-term care insurance: Purchase at age 55
Disability	$50,000–$300,000	Disability insurance: Purchase in 60s, if high risk: personal history of stroke, diabetes, hypertension, heart attack, cancer, or Alzheimer's
Extended longevity (living to 90)	$100,000–$200,000	Annuities or retirement savings[a]
Extended longevity (living to 95)	$200,000–$300,000	Annuities or retirement savings
Uninsured healthcare costs	$200,000–$500,000	Healthcare or catastrophic insurance
Death of wage earner	Salary over term of working life	Life insurance: 6 to 10 times annual salary

Note:
[a]Max out your 401(k) Plan or 403(b) Plan for $15,500 a year. If older than 50, add an extra $5,000 annually.

Life Calculator Exercise TWO: The Value of the Life Calculator

The dollar value the Life Calculator derives from its ability to help you measure the effect of strategies that mitigate the cost of adverse events that affect your balance sheet. By recognizing these effects, you will be able to choose your actions and reduce those costs. The totaled costs in Table 1.5 will be the personal value of the Life Calculator for you.

With the right amount of determination, financial expertise, and hard work, you, too, can become a millionaire. However, as you saw previously, $1 million can quickly disappear, along with your dream of financial independence and security.

The following chapters will educate you in the new risks that you face today, the areas in which you are exposed financially, and the effects that these risks will have on your balance sheet. This book will educate you on strategies, provide technical financial planning tools, and, through the Life Calculator software and Web site, create an environment that encourages you to take the steps necessary to make your millions—and keep them.

The Four Rules of Making Millions

A smart fiscal strategy requires a defined purpose and an accurate assessment of assets and liabilities. You must have a willingness to perform a comprehensive fiscal checkup exposing your financial vulnerability: your savings gap, poor spending habits, failure to protect against downside risk, and ill-timed investment decisions.

Getting a clear view of your future is a start to financial security. Current financial planning books either are written from a policy perspective, documenting in painful statistical detail the decline of economic security, or are cheerleading versions purporting to teach you how to earn millions through various investment schemes.

Moving Up to Millions: The Life Calculator Guide to Building Wealth is a hybrid. It provides a path to personal wealth through over

100 interesting, conversation-stopping facts and 20 Life Calculator exercises by fully integrating the answers to each exercise into a comprehensive financial plan.

The reader will be exposed to 10 hypothetical profiles discussing the challenges of individuals and families from different ages ranging from the decades of the 40s to the 70s. This highly interactive approach guarantees that you can create a winning game plan to secure your financial future and to, perhaps, even earn those millions of dollars, if you take the actions necessary to overcome life's adverse financial events. Through the sophisticated yet easy-to-use digital financial engine you will be in charge of creating an unlimited number of personalized, real-time what-if? scenarios that will optimize your financial success.

The Life Calculator is built on the basic assumption that controlling risk is vital to financial security. There are Four Rules to Financial Success.

Rule #1: Own Your Future

When Enron went bankrupt, Ken and Mary Blackberry, both employed in high-level financial positions, lost not only their jobs, but also their pensions. Not that anyone cared enough to help. It has become a sadly accepted fact that promises made to management are more important than those made to workers. Being older workers (Ken was 60 and Mary was 54), the Blackberrys had little time left to recover their pension losses, but they were not deterred. They quickly adapted, selling their expensive home in Houston and moving to Austin, where housing and living expenses were substantially cheaper. Mary Blackberry went to work as a CPA for a state agency. Ken now serves as a financial consultant. Both have adopted the attitude that their future is their own responsibility.

Hank and Trudy Trio are similarly making it on their own. Both union workers, the Trios were accustomed to self-reliance, hard work, and long hours. Trudy was employed in the hospitality industry, while Hank worked in construction. While raising five children, they carefully budgeted and managed to save for their retirement, take care of their aging parents, and set up a health savings account to serve as a resource for Trudy's diabetic care. They were fortunate to have the live-in support of Trudy's mother, saving the expenses of child care that would have otherwise been prohibitive and would have prevented Trudy from bringing in a second income.

The Trios and the Blackberrys are symbolic of Rule #1: Own Your Future, recognizing that neither employers nor government may provide the expected degree of support. Take the lead role in managing your balance sheet, creating a plan to protect against a multitude of adverse events that may impact your future.

Rule #2: Focus on Reducing Risk

Eric Router, a real estate appraiser from Portland, Oregon, is employed on contract by a large real estate brokerage company to appraise estates, apartments, and small commercial buildings. Eric is proud of his real estate knowledge and has leveraged it to purchase a series of single-family homes and a small eight-unit apartment building, all at substantial market discounts due to bankruptcy sales. Router made attractive returns on his real estate portfolio until he encountered three unexpected issues:

1. A drop in residential values in a neighborhood due to recently announced highway construction
2. Litigation costs with tenants regarding damaged personal property due to leakage from recent storms
3. A drop in values in his overall portfolio leading to a highly leveraged position

Router's personal life was marked by recent unfunded healthcare costs for emergency room treatment following a serious rock-climbing accident and a knee injury some years earlier. Prior to this medical incident, he had always been in outstanding health and was a mountain climber, marathon runner, and downhill skier. He had chosen not to purchase healthcare insurance, gambling that the $4,000 to $7,000 annual payment for healthcare premiums was better spent invested in his real estate transactions. Subsequent to his real estate losses and medical costs, Router has reduced his risk by rebalancing his portfolio, purchasing alumni healthcare insurance from his university program, and selling selected real estate properties to invest the proceeds in mutual funds and conservative blue-chip stocks.

Marla and Bill Newton, former entrepreneurs from Atlanta, Georgia, have experience in reducing their risk. Marla determined to stay at home with their children, while Bill engaged in entrepreneurial activity, forming a real estate investment trust (REIT) with his brother. Bill discovered, as an aspiring entrepreneur, that while his compensation might be significantly higher than a salaried position, the income volatility was also higher. Seeking to build a consistent stream of income, Bill become employed as a real estate manager for a large corporation and Marla transitioned to employment as a guidance counselor for a local high school. Both Bill and Marla enjoy the healthcare insurance and pension benefits of their new positions.

Reducing risk was more important than maximizing return to both Router and the Newtons. The Newtons reduced their risk by taking jobs with employer-provided pensions and healthcare, and Router reduced his risk by purchasing healthcare insurance and diversifying his portfolio into equity, bonds, and mutual funds. Both sets of decisions are wise, recognizing the importance of managing risk over maximizing return.

Life Calculator Exercise THREE: Risk Management

Analyze the impact of a 2 percent higher return on your portfolio. Would a 2 percent return provide sufficient savings to finance the two most likely adverse events that will occur over the next 10 years of your life? Please note the adverse events table in Chapter 3 and log on to www.LifeCalculator.Net, following the link on the Risk Management Exercise.

Rule #3: Make Time Your Ally

Adriana Dell is a nurse who discovered, after her divorce, why women are the most likely to be impoverished. Adriana had no retirement savings and, with her small income, no hope of building a sizable nest egg. However, as a nurse, she did have one advantage over most workers. Her healthcare costs, usually one of the largest costs for older workers, were relatively low because of her employment. After considering alternative employers, Dell joined a hospital chain that offered an employer-matched savings plan. The growth of her savings, doubled by her employer match, helped to ensure her financial security, making time her ally.

Peter and Betty Moto were well on their way to achieving their financial goals when disaster occurred. Their 23-year-old uninsured son was involved in a car accident, necessitating enormous hospital bills and three years of costly rehabilitation. However, the Motos had always been prudent in their financial practices, investing the maximum allowable in their employer-matched savings program. At the time of their son's injury, they were able to divert a portion of their personal savings into an emergency fund to support his care and recovery.

The Motos had carefully planned for over two decades for early retirement, which they now sacrificed to ensure the highest-quality medical care for their son. By maintaining a safety margin in their personal finances, the Motos had ultimate financial flexibility in meeting unexpected adverse events. With Peter's willingness to work an extended period beyond his retirement, the Motos were able to replace much of their personal savings.

Delaying financial planning with the expectation of a future windfall, a salary increase, or even an inheritance that will magically erase your savings gap will leave you at a substantial time disadvantage. Time is an ally, if you take the actions to protect against the negative outcomes of adverse events by buying insurance policies, by compounding long-term investments, and by delaying retirement to accumulate additional assets and in forestalling spending retirement resources.

Rule #4: Master Change

Dan Apple from New York was extremely frustrated. His previously secure finances had been exactly halved after his divorce, and, additionally, he now had to support his new wife and child. Attempting to leverage his substantially reduced investment portfolio, he placed a significant portion into a hedge fund, only to lose over a third of it.

To recover from his reduced financial position, Dan determined to work until 70, and his young wife accepted the necessity of employment once their child was of school age. Reducing their budget, downsizing their home, and focusing on longer-term objectives rather than short-term enjoyment was a difficult transition. Their ability to master those changes will make the difference in their extended financial security.

The Palms have only recently realized the uncertainty of life. Jack Palm, a Silicon Valley programmer, has experienced two interim jobs following his unexpected dismissal from his senior position as a computer programmer. Jack returned to community college to complete a master's degree and to receive a professional certificate, valued in his field.

With his additional credentials and a willingness to accept a much-reduced salary and title, Jack has found permanent employment in a midsize company that is certain to not offshore his position. His reduced income has required the family to alter their spending, decrease the amount they can spend on college educations, and curtail purchases of expensive foreign cars and a second home.

Your life is not static. Neither is your financial plan. You must continually respond to events that occur in your life and revise your plan, if needed.

2

Threats to Millionaire Status

Few of us stop to consider how our financial circumstances have changed over the years. These realizations typically occur suddenly, perhaps at an important birthday, when we notice that our current lifestyle is not as we had assumed it would be when we were younger. Some of you may have received this siren call when you realized that you did not have sufficient financial resources to both live the expensive lifestyle that you had always envisioned *and* to retire comfortably. As the years pass and we are absorbed by the challenges of finishing our education, getting our first job, receiving our first promotion, enjoying the leverage of credit cards, starting a family, and perhaps purchasing our first house, few of us step back to examine whether we are on track to achieve our personal and financial goals.

Our energies are totally committed to living in the present, to mastering our current challenges and responding to new opportunities. Rarely do we have the luxury of unprogrammable time away from the hectic schedules that dictate our lives.

Take a moment and reflect. Your life is remarkably different from that of your parents. Many of your parents have the benefit of secure lifelong employment, complete with a defined-benefit plan and comprehensive healthcare. Most of your parents benefited from a remarkable appreciation in the housing market and owned their homes free and clear of any debt before they retired. This home equity, together with their defined-benefit plans, enabled tens of thousands of middle-class Americans to become millionaires—if only on paper.

The generations of those aged 35 to 60 are faced with new threats to achieving financial security: extended longevity, under-funded pensions, increased concerns regarding the stability of Social Security, the elimination of defined benefits for most careers, growing healthcare expenses that are less likely to be funded by an employer, soaring college costs, and lack of personal savings. For us, the route to millionaire and multimillionaire status will require much greater knowledge and initiative, as we will not be able to rely on the security of employer-sponsored pensions or, perhaps, even a fully funded Social Security system. It is less likely that we will have the generous benefits of an employer-subsidized healthcare plan. Moreover, increased globalization threatens job security in ways that our parents never envisioned when they entered the workforce.

This book, together with its Life Calculator software program, will empower you to become your own financial advisor, drawing on the resources of an enormous database of financial information, the unique opportunity to create and test alternative financial strategies, and the ability to measure the impact of various life events on your financial security. You will be able to become your own financial advisor, guiding your own progress to secure financial goals.

Why Your Life Cycle Is Not Like Your Parents'

The new realities that define your life cycle as distinctly different from that of your parents include:

- A 24-hour Web-connected world shaped by globalization, where politics, education, and communication are instantaneous.
- Upper-middle-class families experience the same income instability as blue-collar workers.
- A standard employment profile is of people working to 70 years of age or longer.

- The empty-nester status will disappear as elderly parents are cared for under the same roof as returning post–college-graduate children.

In addition, the entire concept of *retirement* is retired. You now face the reality that as you live longer, save less money, and remain healthier, it will be necessary to redefine a reasonable retirement schedule—one that is personalized.

Your retirement plan could also be affected by dramatic shifts in U.S. attitudes and confidence regarding the future. Your parents' generation, known as the *Silent Generation* if born before 1946, survived both the Great Depression and World War II. They have a remarkable level of savings, are benefiting from company-provided pensions, and, until recently, never experienced the fear of not being able to afford healthcare.

According to recent 2006 electoral exit polls, you are the first American generation that has a larger percentage of respondents (40 percent) stating that they expect life for the next generation of Americans to be worse than the present, with only 30 percent expecting it to be better. Reinforcing this attitude are the 55 percent of Americans who believe "things are seriously off on the wrong track" versus the 41 percent who think "things are going in the right direction."[1] You are the first American generation who might not attain the American dream, having a better life than what was typical for your parents.

These are just opinions, however. Regardless of whether you share a positive or pessimistic outlook on your financial situation or the future economy, your financial plan will be affected by major structural shifts that distinguish your life cycle from that of your parents. Among the most important issues are longevity, multigenerational caregiving, savings rate, pensions and Social Security benefits, and healthcare costs.

Extended Longevity

Increased longevity, more than any other factor, defines your life cycle as distinct from your parents. (See Figure 2.1.)

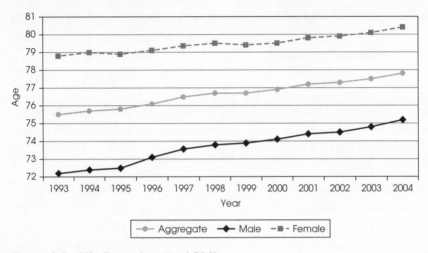

Figure 2.1 Life Expectancy at Birth

Source: Data compiled from Life Tables, National Center for Health Statistics, www.cdc.gov/nchs/

When Social Security was initially passed in 1935, it was expected that Americans would live to age 63, resulting in many individuals never drawing down on Social Security. Today, individuals can expect to live to 78,[2] 15 years longer than their counterparts in 1935. Almost two out of five (39 percent) of today's 60-year-old males and over half (53 percent) of 60-year-old women will live to age 90. You might be surprised that over one out of five men (22 percent) and almost one out of three women (30 percent) will celebrate their ninety-fifth birthday. A woman's life expectancy is three years longer than a man's at age 65, and almost three-quarters of the population is female after age 85.[3] This is illustrated in Table 2.1.

Life Calculator Exercise FOUR: Longevity

Log on to the Web site www.LifeCalculator.Net and follow the link to the Longevity Exercise that projects your expected life span.

Table 2.1   Probabilities of Longevity

	Probabilities of Living to Different Ages*							
	Living to 80		Living to 85		Living to 90		Living to 95	
Currently	Male	Female	Male	Female	Male	Female	Male	Female
60	73%	83%	58%	70%	39%	52%	22%	30%
65	75%	84%	60%	71%	41%	53%	22%	31%
70	79%	87%	63%	74%	43%	54%	23%	32%

	Probability of Both Living to This Age[a]			
Current Age	80	85	90	95
60	61%	41%	20%	7%
65	63%	43%	22%	7%
70	69%	47%	23%	7%

	Probability of Both Dying by This Age			
Current Age	80	85	90	95
60	5%	13%	29%	55%
65	4%	12%	28%	54%
70	3%	10%	26%	52%

	Probability of at Least One Person Living to This Age			
Current Age	80	85	90	95
60	35%	47%	50%	39%
65	33%	46%	51%	39%
70	29%	44%	51%	40%

Note:

[a] Assuming that mortality probabilities for both men and women are independent, the probability of a couple (male and female) living to a certain age is the product of the probability of each living to that age. The probability of both dying by that age is the product of the probabilities that each die by that age or (1 – (Probability of each living to that age)) × (1 – (Probability of each living to that age)). The probability of at least one person living to that age is the remainder, so that all the probabilities sum to one.

*Source: 2003 TIAA Mortality Tables.

The next time you are at a community event or business conference, look across the row of people seated next to you and reflect on those statistics. Reference these statistics at a backyard barbecue or over cocktails and you will confirm that few Americans are informed of the changed demographics. Only a very small percentage of Americans have consciously factored potentially living to 95 into their investment and retirement planning.

Multigenerational Caregiving Responsibilities

American families will now have to face another consequence of longevity. Known as the *Sandwich Generation,* 40 percent of Americans between the ages of 40 and 60 (baby boomers) are now supporting a child under the age of 25 *and* supporting a parent or grandparent.[4] Within 10 years, more than two-thirds of them are expected to take care of an elderly parent. With smaller savings, increasing levels of debt, declining equity in their principal residence, and limited employer support for retirement, few individuals or families are able to assume the increased financial load of caregiving.

> The baby boomers will be the first generation to spend more years caring for aging parents than they do raising their own children.

For a growing subset of individuals and families who experience caregiving obligations for three generations of family (their parents, children, and grandchildren), a *Club Sandwich* effect occurs, with serious impact on the principal individual or family who reallocates its resources, emotionally and financially, to meet the needs of multiple generations. The principal who is responsible for funding the club sandwich arrangement loses the sense of freedom that comes from being an empty nester, while assuming the financial pressures of multiple households.

Many midlife households are faced with an uncomfortable decision: Do they deplete their retirement accounts to care for an elderly parent? With care of elderly parents expected to cost $7,000 annually, if the parent resides at home with you,[5] or more than $75,000, if at a nursing home,[6] the decision to provide partial or total supportmay well jeopardize your retirement comfort. The care of multiple parents may threaten the very foundation of your retirement security.

Readers are advised to perform the Life Calculator exercise on caregiving in this chapter to appreciate the long-term financial impact of depleting their savings prior to retirement. Refer to the section on caregiving in Chapters 4 and 7 for further discussion regarding this issue.

Care of an elderly parent is only half of the sandwich generation's challenge. Equally expensive is the support of their children, both in college and often post college when they return home, as increasing numbers of young adults are unable to become financially independent. Again, the midlife couple must balance the imperative to save for retirement while contributing to the support of their children—and perhaps even helping pay off their children's college debt, averaging $30,000 for a public university.[7]

Life Calculator Exercise FIVE: Caregiving

Log on to the Web site www.LifeCalculator.Net to perform the Caregiving Exercise, which will enable you to create a caregiver budget for a family member, factoring the person's age, life expectancy, medical conditions, type of living facility and geographic location.

Low Savings

Although longevity and multigenerational caregiving are distinguishing factors explaining why your life cycle is not your parents', the level of personal savings is a third element that distinguishes those midlife readers, ages 40 to 60, from previous generations. From 1952 through 1994, savings rates averaged 8 percent to 10 percent of personal income. From 1995 to 2000, savings rates dropped dramatically to 5 percent, with the rates averaging 2 percent from 2000 to 2004. In 2005, the

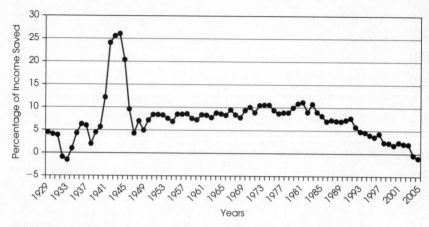

Figure 2.2 **Personal Saving as a Percentage of Disposable Personal Income**

Source: 2005 Bureau of Economic Analysis, National Income and Product Accounts (NIPA) "Table 2.1 Personal Income and Its Disposition," www.bea.gov/national/nipaweb/index.asp

savings rate dropped to −0.4 percent, a negative savings level for the first time since the Great Depression in the 1930s. (See Figure 2.2.)

Given the stronger economy in recent years, a generally positive business outlook, and the rapidly appreciating housing market, the negative savings rate is difficult to justify. Some of the fault undoubtedly can be attributed to a consumer mentality that is reluctant to defer purchasing the latest fashion or technology and fails to establish even a general budget for household expenses. However, this consumer mentality does not fully explain the low saving rate in an apparently healthy economy.

Families and individuals have been assaulted with a number of developments that have decreased savings. Among the notable ones are increasingly costly healthcare premiums, higher college tuition, accelerating energy costs, and overinvestment in housing.

The frustration of many Americans regarding their ability to improve their economic security is sadly confirmed by the view of one out of five Americans in 2006 that winning the lottery, not saving or investing, is the most practical way to accumulate wealth.[8]

The low savings rate is confirmed by the glaring statistics in the list that follows. With three out of four Americans over age 55 reporting less than $250,000 in assets, and only 12 percent of workers of all ages reporting that asset level, there is an urgent need to address the problem regarding savings levels, particularly in a political environment that has transferred the responsibility for retirement security to the individual.

- 27 percent of households with a head of household aged 47 to 64 are approaching retirement with expected retirement income of less than half of their current income.[9]
- 65 percent of U.S. households in 2006 have accumulated less than $50,000 in savings; 12 percent have saved only $50,000 to $100,000.
- 50 percent of workers over 55 years of age have saved $50,000 or less, not including their principal residence. Of that age group, 12 percent also report savings of $50,000 to $100,000.
- In contrast, 26 percent of workers over 55 have succeeded in accumulating $250,000 or higher in assets, with one-half

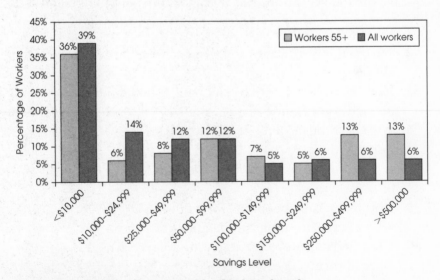

Figure 2.3 Workers Separated by Savings Level

Source: Ruth Helman, Matthew Greenwald & Associates, Craig Copeland and Jack VanDerhei, "Will More of Us Be Working Forever? The 2006 Retirement Confidence Survey," Employee Benefit Research Institute

of that group (13 percent) claiming $500,000 or more in savings.

- For workers of all ages, the numbers are half of that level, with only 12 percent reporting assets over $250,000, and 6 percent reporting assets over $500,000.[10]

Cracks in Social Security and Pension Support

A major source of financial anxiety for Americans is their retirement finances. With limited savings and high levels of personal debt, the average American is increasingly dependent on both Social Security and employer-sponsored pensions to support their preferred lifestyles in retirement. However, such dependence is not realistic, given that Social Security is meager and employers are increasingly freezing or defaulting on their pension obligations. Personal responsibility and privatization are being offered as policy alternatives to employer-supported retirement plans and a fully funded Social Security system, but their consequences on a generation unprepared to take financial responsibility will be deadly.

Take the following quiz. Answers are at the bottom of page 33.

1. What is the average balance in a 401(k)?
2. What is the typical annual Social Security payment in 2007 for couples?
3. How many workers have neither a defined-benefit nor a defined-contribution plan?
4. What percentage of the nation's small businesses fail to provide workers with:
   a. Any retirement benefit?
   b. Access to a 401(k)?
5. How many baby boomers working for S&P 500 corporations will be at risk for underfunded pension funds?
6. What percentage of the following will receive 50 percent or more of their retirement income from Social Security?[11]
   a. Couples
   b. Singles
   c. Senior women

7. What percentage of the following will receive 90 percent or more of their retirement income from Social Security?[12]
   a. Couples
   b. Singles
   c. Senior women
8. What is the approximate percentage of Social Security benefits that women receive compared to men?

How many of your answers were correct? These statistics should be a code red for readers who keep deferring taking action to ensure their own financial security.

Although Social Security benefits are not expected to be depleted until 2040, a more critical issue for those over 40 is the limited supplemental support that Social Security contributes to a comfortable retirement. The decline in employer-supported retirement plans only aggravates the sense of financial insecurity experienced by many readers. See Figure 2.4.

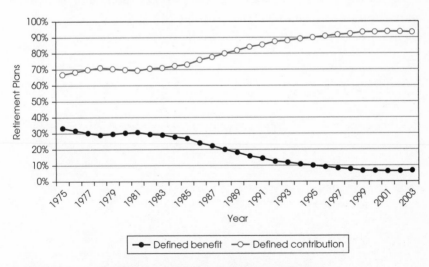

Figure 2.4 Percentage of Existing Retirement Plans

Source: Data compiled by author from various private pension plan bulletins, form 5500. United States Department of Labor, Pension and Welfare Benefits Administration

Answers: (1) $58,328; (2) $20,556; (3) 40 percent; (4a) 63 percent; (4b) 14 percent; (5) 81 percent; (6a) 50 percent; (6b) 75 percent; (6c) 75 percent; (7a) 20 percent; (7b) 40 percent; (7c) 44 percent; and (8) 50 percent.

Expectations regarding quality of life in retirement dropped sharply, from 52 percent of workers in 2004 to 38 percent in 2006 who state that they believe they will live as well or better in retirement as when working.[13]

Growing Healthcare Costs

As you grow older, your spending priorities will change. To meet a shrinking income, you will begin to spend less in all categories except healthcare, for which spending increases as age increases. Unfortunately, most people spend less on personal insurance when they need it the most—when they are older and when their savings cannot afford to take the brunt of any catastrophic event. (See Figure 2.5.)

These facts portend an ominous trend. Americans are woefully unprepared for their futures, yet, they are being asked to bear a greater amount of financial risk in their life as their employers reduce healthcare benefits. (See Figure 2.6.)

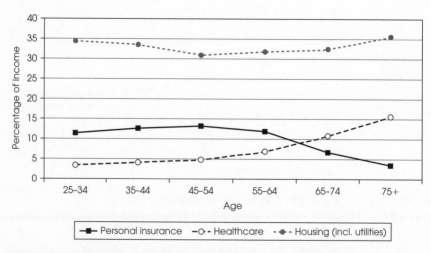

Figure 2.5 Spending on Items as a Percentage of Income

Source: U.S. Department of Labor, "Consumer Expenditures in 2005" (February 2007), U.S. Bureau of Labor Statistics, Report 998

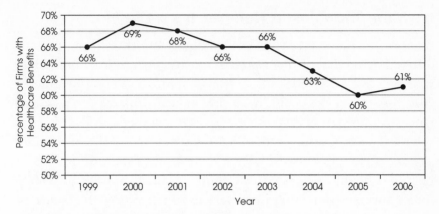

Figure 2.6   Percentage of Firms Offering Health Benefits

Source: "Employer Health Benefits, 2006 Annual Survey," Kaiser Family Foundation and Health Research & Educational Trust, www.kff.org/insurance/7527/upload7527.pdf

Summing It Up

Your life cycle is not like that of your parents: you are faced with more choices and less financial resources. Many of you are being asked to use your own judgment on how to invest your 401(k) savings; increasing numbers are having to identify their own healthcare plans and negotiate premiums; and some will have to trade off their own retirement security in order to fund their parents or children. Unfortunately, we are living in a society where Social Security, pension, and healthcare systems have not adjusted to the changed world. Companies are shedding their pensions, cutting back on health benefits, and reorganizing the employer-employee relationship. Your parents' financial security was characterized by a steady pension and generous healthcare benefits. You will not be so lucky.

More and more readers will be forced to rethink the traditional notion of a comfortable retirement. Many will have to continue working well beyond 65 in order to finance the care of their loved ones, provide needed retirement income, offset the loss of pensions, and pay for the costs of adverse events, such as divorce and uninsured healthcare costs. Lack of retirement security also may necessitate them working well into their 70s.

It's More Than Just a Number, It's a Life Plan

By now you know that your own financial future will be distinctly different from that of your parents. You are likely to live longer than your parents; have reduced pensions, rapidly escalating healthcare costs, limited savings, and, most probably, no chance of an inheritance, as your parents will live longer than planned.

You could have more than a 50 percent probability of personally experiencing at least 2 of the 12 life's adverse events identified next and further discussed in Chapter 4. Based on the probabilities of adverse events that you might experience over the course of your life, you might incur financial losses of $250,000 to $500,000. If you are unfortunate enough to experience a higher number of adverse events, and if you have not taken the pragmatic actions recommended in this book to reduce your risk, your financial losses may well exceed $1 million. The good news is that you will be able to mitigate most of these costs with proactive financial planning and risk management.

The "Number"

Many financial planning and retirement guides propagate the myth that there is a *number*—the amount of savings needed to support you and your family in a comfortable retirement. The obsession with identifying the number adheres to an outdated approach that focuses on a single moment in time and freezes all market information and portfolio allocations.

A more sophisticated approach, called *Monte Carlo modeling*, attempts to create a dynamic forecast using simulations that reflect a range of probabilities, investment returns, inflation, and asset performance data. The results of a Monte Carlo model are generally portrayed in a matrix of investment possibilities that indicate the probability of you reaching specific financial milestones, which may require you to reallocate your investment assets.

The limitation of Monte Carlo simulations is the inability to integrate personal life-cycle information into their investment analysis. Your need to care for an aging parent, a sudden uninsured healthcare crisis, an unexpected family expense, or a loss of job, among other personal variables, are not factored into a Monte Carlo simulation.

Financial engine tools currently do not have the capacity to address these events and lack any ability to assign probabilities to adverse events that may disrupt your investment planning. Such analytical tools fail to prepare you for the potential negative impacts of personal adverse events.

The Life Calculator is unique in performing a 360-degree review of your world, integrating financial simulations with both current and projected life events. The Life Calculator will enable you to select any combination of What-If? scenarios, determining the impact on your balance sheet.

What If you suffer a job loss at age 45 or 50? How do you balance an underfunded pension, caregiving expenses, and extended longevity? Are you better advised over a 15-year period to buy a smaller, less-expensive home and invest the savings in the stock market, or purchase a larger home and bet on high home appreciation? How much long-term care insurance should you buy, and when? Does a reverse mortgage make sense, given your personal priorities? Whatever combination of scenarios you wish to test, the Life Calculator will figure financial outcomes, providing a valuable tool for managing risk and improving returns.

The Life Calculator is the only customized, comprehensive online program designed to create detailed financial strategies to ensure your financial security. Its worksheets offer valuable assistance:

- You can do unlimited What-If? scenarios, integrating your investment strategy with real-life events by varying market return, volatility, retirement age, career status, and adverse events.
- Powerful probability analysis tools allow you to gauge the odds of adverse events impacting your life.
- You can get advice on asset allocation and stress-test investment strategies.
- Retirement savings gaps can be calculated.

- The program offers assistance in budgeting expenses, including college education, caregiver expenses, healthcare, mortgage, and insurance.
- Life Calculator will serve as your personal financial balance sheet, providing secure encrypted digital storage for your financial information.

As you create alternative personal profiles, you can save your financial plans online in an individual file, allowing you to access them whenever desired.

Let's Get Started—Becoming Your Own Financial Advisor

You are now employed as your own personal financial advisor. Congratulations on your new assignment! Welcome to your new office at www.LifeCalculator.Net, available to you 24/7 from anywhere you may travel.

Included in this book are 10 hypothetical profiles varied by income, profession, lifestyle, geography, and adverse events. They are true reflections of individuals and families who have been interviewed in preparation of this book. This book also provides access to seven Life Calculator exercises, ranging from assessing your weaknesses to goal setting and strategy implementation.

With the purchase of this book, you have a 30-day complimentary membership to the LifeCalculator.Net Web site. On that Web site is a customized version of the Life Calculator that offers you online access to the profiles and to the seven financial planning exercises included in this book. Upon use of the Life Calculator.Net services, you may choose to continue your services and upgrade to an extensive range of data sources, participate in the expert panels on topics of financial planning and investment interest, and access the expanded library of profiles and 20 financial planning exercises. Importantly, the Life Calculator has a comprehensive library of the following:

- Healthcare matters, including incidence of illnesses and average healthcare spending by age

- Job information on growth industries, benefits, and salary
- Real estate appreciation trends, assisted living, and cooperative housing information
- Tax-friendly states and costs of living by state
- Hyperlinks to over a hundred informational and helpful Web sources
- Investment returns by asset categories
- Social Security and Pension Benefit Guaranty Corporation (PBGC) benefit data and inflation rates

Full membership on LifeCalculator.Net offers the opportunity to create individualized What-If analysis, creating unlimited combinations of adverse events and determining the impact on your financial and retirement security. The Life Calculator will immediately display your resulting savings gap and identify at what age your savings will be depleted.

You are advised to be a frequent user of these resources, which will provide immediate updates of financial news, market information, and topical issues. Engage in the discussion and panels and volunteer your own experiences. Serve as a mentor to others and gain from their knowledge.

You are now empowered to begin your journey toward financial independence, equipped with the sophisticated tools of LifeCalculator.Net to assist you in evaluating life choices and in creating best-case scenarios for your economic future. With consistent commitment, you will be able to deal effectively with today's financial concerns and will be prepared to conquer tomorrow's future challenges. You will have the wisdom, the insight, and the confidence to see through every personal decision you need to make.

3

Click Your Way to Personal Wealth

Whether you are earning $50,000 or $250,000 a year, *you* can achieve a comfortable level of financial security. Quality of life is not solely defined by net worth—it is determined by the proactive decisions you make.

Living a comfortable life—enjoying the activities that bring you pleasure; supporting your children in achieving their goals and your parents in maintaining their lifestyle; experiencing a sense of achievement in your work; cherishing your community of friends and neighbors—these are the cornerstones of an enviable life. There is great freedom in having the flexibility to engage in new careers, either by choice or by necessity, and knowing that you have sufficient financial resources for your older years.

You must take charge of your financial future! Lamenting the loss of a job, an underfunded pension, unexpected health expenses, care of an aging parent, and ballooning college bills will not change your bottom line. Nor will anxious hours spent reading advice on investing—if you don't understand your own financial profile. Be clear about your financial goals and learn how to prepare yourself for adverse events that may prevent you from enjoying a comfortable life.

The Three Es of Financial Planning

Every day brings new announcements of pension shortfalls and deci-sions by companies such as IBM, Verizon, Motorola, and Sears to no longer fund employee pension plans. They are joining the growing number of businesses that have shifted responsibility to their em-ployees for making financial provisions for retirement. Millions of baby boomers are now attempting to manage their retirement sav-ings through various types of 401(k) plans, and they are facing the reality that they are truly on their own. However, the job need not be overwhelming. Mastering your financial future is as simple as apply-ing the three Es of financial planning.

Evaluation

What is your savings gap, and where are your financial vulnerabilities, both currently and in the identifiable future? *Evaluate your personal financial situation and calculate how much money you will need to reach your goals.* You will be able to determine exact savings goals for each life-cycle period, with the ultimate goal of targeting an amount of re-tirement savings that will enable you to have the lifestyle you desire, while meeting all the challenges discussed in this book.

The Life Calculator will help you create a range of scenarios from which to select your targeted savings goal, one custom-tailored to your own set of investment assumptions, lifestyle choices, and per-sonal obligations. As you encounter new challenges that change your perspective on your priorities, you can instantly revise your financial plan simply by inputting new information.

Education

What do you need to know, and where can you find reliable infor-mation on investments, the economy, healthcare and tax policies, real estate values, employment, and career outlooks? *Educate yourself about the changing financial dynamics of your world through the daily use of LifeCalculator.Net* to update your understanding of financial markets, economics, and policies that will affect your future. Use the over 100 hyperlinks to explore career, healthcare, and investment sources. Update yourself on market trends. Keep yourself informed about changing federal and state tax policies, and track housing prices in your community.

Execution

Do you know the importance of market timing on your investment decisions, including the purchase and sale of real estate? Have you performed alternative sensitivity analysis to determine the best-case scenario? *Execute a plan that will track the changes you have decided to make to achieve greater financial resources.* Act without delay to execute decisions, review the outcome of your actions, and modify your plan as changes in your life and the world around you dictate.

Power Your Future: The Life Calculator Is Your Personal Financial Advisor

Most people have mixed reactions to financial planning: they defer it to another year because of apprehensions about what they might learn about their financial status. Or they conclude that it is just too complicated to understand on their own. They are repelled by the expensive up-front fees and monthly service charges required by the numerous investment and financial planning services. Moreover, they suspect that many of those offering such financial planning advice are pushing their own financial products.

All of these reactions are understandable. Basic financial calculators, available through dozens of online Web sites and organizations, offer simple financial planning—without factoring in your personal financial challenges or potential changes in lifestyle. These flat-line programs are one-dimensional—they do not give you the capability to carry out either dynamic analysis or life cycle planning. Although they can offer you a ballpark estimate of your finances today, they do not educate you about the financial impact of your decisions, realistically measure volatility and inflation, enable you to test multiple competitive investment strategies, engage in life-cycle planning, or provide a tool to continually update your financial status.

The Digital Toolbox

This book is accompanied by a toolbox of digital financial resources available at www.LifeCalculator.Net. The basic Life Calculator is intended for those readers who simply wish to address basic financial planning, including savings, debt, and investment goals. The deluxe Life Calculator, a sophisticated financial engine, empowers those readers who wish to create a comprehensive financial analysis, integrating both positive and negative future changes in their lifestyle and financial resources. Importantly, the deluxe Life Calculator program will educate you on potential strategies to offset adverse events.

You will also be able to access the LifeCalculator.Net Web site for updated financial and market information. The Web site provides a forum for those desiring to exchange information with others. It offers weekly webcasts with panels of financial experts on strategies to enhance your financial security.

Smart-Advice Financial Engines

Understand the value of *dynamic* financial planning. No financial calculator has previously been available that performs *dynamic analysis* on a personalized basis, a calculator capable of creating a financial plan that can be updated by you, as you experience both positive and negative changes in your lifestyle. These changes might include a job promotion, unexpected inheritance, the diagnosis of an expensive medical problem, an underfunded pension, or a costly divorce, to name only a few possible life experiences.

Smart-advice financial engines such as the Life Calculator are a second generation of more sophisticated proprietary computer programs that incorporate thousands of simulations while adjusting for a myriad of factors: inflation, interest rates, investment returns, duration of investment, and asset allocation. These engines conduct dynamic planning, providing upside and downside scenarios, minimum and maximum ranges needed for financial security and retirement, detailed asset allocation options, risk tolerance measures, and even offer estate planning services.

The drawback? They are available through financial planning and investment management services only to those who have investment accounts of more than a quarter of a million dollars or who are willing to pay a minimum $1,000 fee for a one-time snapshot of their financial status. The Life Calculator is an online financial advisor that is not tied to investment, insurance, or banking services. It provides independent, customized advice without the expectations that the user will purchase affiliated investment products.

Adverse Events Probabilities

The Life Calculator performs sophisticated dynamic analysis, taking you from where you are today to where you wish to be at various points in your future life cycles. It identifies the major threats to your personal financial security, suggests recovery strategies, and provides an anxiety-free roadmap to follow throughout the planning process, as your life journey takes unexpected twists. This is made possible when you simply input new data and analyze the results. It is your free virtual financial advisor—always available wherever you are—providing you with a vast range of simulations of possible financial scenarios.

Life-Cycle Planning

Life-cycle planning takes into account many more factors than traditional retirement planning. It offers its users the ability to incorporate alternative work and personal lifestyle futures that they outline, which may include working longer, taking a sabbatical and then returning to work, exploring virtual employment with multiple clients, or retraining for newer technologies.

Life-cycle planning, available through the Life Calculator, also incorporates the specific age-related family and personal priorities that characterize the evolving stages of your life (see Chapters 8 and 9).

Customized What-if Scenarios

It is vital that you actively prepare for your future, recognizing the dramatically different world described in the previous chapter. You will be digitally connected to a global society whose demographics and economies will impact your own lifestyle. Simply knowing your current financial health fails to ensure that you will take necessary actions to maximize your financial future and protect against life's inevitable adverse turns.

The Life Calculator has been created with simple layout and tab features that will take you through the steps required to create a basic or most probable scenario, one that can be modified with countless variations, that anticipates future developments—both positive and negative.

Comparative Portfolio Evaluation

In the investment arena, the Life Calculator helps you create a number of different portfolios, with investment mixes adjusted for risk tolerance to reflect your changing life-cycle priorities. It factors in inflation, volatility, savings and debt levels, pension contributions, Social Security payments, and income sources. (In Chapter 4, economic variables such as inflation and volatility, which can severely reduce investment returns, are discussed in depth.)

Testing Alternative Scenarios

The asset allocation scenarios are integrated with your personal financial profile and economic variables to help you design your three baseline financial forecasts—a most-likely scenario, a worst-case scenario, and an optimum outcome. Unlike the commercial financial engines, the Life Calculator does not provide specific investment advice. This program enables you to create your own investment portfolio after you evaluate its simulations.

The historical returns table, included in Chapter 6 and as a file on LifeCalculator.Net, identifies the range of investment returns that may be considered. If you are uncertain regarding your investment return, the default function of the Life Calculator will automatically assign the historical return targets for all asset classes. You should have a balanced portfolio of assets reflecting your risk tolerance, investment return targets, need for income versus appreciation, and life-cycle period.

Risk Tolerance Profile

The Life Calculator focuses on the trade-off between maintaining wealth at limited risk with lower returns and earning incremental investment gains while assuming higher risk exposure. As you read this book and learn about life-cycle planning, you will be able to determine your risk tolerance—a very personal decision that should be made after full consideration of your retirement goals; your expected length of employment; total savings; family responsibilities for the financial support of your parents, relatives, children, and grandchildren; and expected longevity.

How to Start

What do you need before accessing the Life Calculator to start creating your plan?

You must collect all your financial data: Social Security information; pension funding; personal savings, investments; employer-matched programs; fixed expenses (including insurance, mortgage or rent, utilities, food; and membership dues); variable expenses (clothing, travel, entertainment, tuition, medical); and net current value of home after mortgage. The Life Calculator can be adjusted for varying economic scenarios, including hyperinflation, a range of investment returns, increased savings, debt repayment, and retirement withdrawal levels.

Its customized approach allows you to input essential planning considerations:

- Age at retirement
- Underfunded pension

- Timing of sale of home
- Reverse annuity mortgage
- Unemployment or reduced employment
- Divorce, marriage, or remarriage
- Care of elderly relatives
- Child support and college expenses
- Relocation
- Uninsured health care expenses
- Loss of property due to a natural or man-made disaster

Life Calculator Exercise SIX: Saving or Paying Down Debt?

Should you save or pay down debt? Determine the benefits. Select the Saving or Paying Down Debt Exercise link at www.LifeCalculator.Net for your personalized analysis.

What the Life Calculator Will Show You

When you have completed the process, you will have a very clear idea of the likelihood of your achieving a particular goal, given a set of circumstances you have defined.

For example, can a couple, currently 55, retire at 65, given the following assumptions?

- Joint income of $120,000; after-tax income of $112,000
- 5 percent return on investments of $500,000
- Employer-matched 401(k) for one spouse of 50 cents to a dollar
- Fully paid mortgage
- Care for an elderly parent at home, with $7,000 annual expenses
- College and personal spending of $101,640 annually—resulting in a net savings rate of 3 percent
- Assumed withdrawal rate after retirement of 90 percent of pre-retirement income or $100,800

The Life Calculator will report on their projected assets at retirement age and the age at which those assets will be depleted. If we assume an inflation rate of 3 percent, this couple will have amassed a total of $835,333 at their retirement and will deplete that amount by age 76.

Try It Again and Again, Until Satisfied

If the couple is unhappy with that result—and they certainly will be, since actuarial tables confirm that both spouses will most likely live into their 80s and, perhaps, into their 90s—they may choose to compare alternative strategies. They might have to work longer, take greater risk with their investment portfolio, have their children finance college through loans, increase savings, or downsize to a less expensive home or location.

For example, if they simply defer retirement to age 70, avoid spending retirement savings an additional five years, and, importantly, gain compound interest return on those savings for an additional five years, they will have $1,089,327 at retirement. That amount will last them to age 89—a much more secure financial forecast.

Identify Your Optimum Future

Using the Life Calculator, you can create various futures—all in a matter of minutes. The benefits are immediate: you instantly know both the good and the bad news. Unlike any other financial planning device, you are not charged for repeated scenarios—you can continue to refine your strategy until you are satisfied with your financial plan. You can return to use the Life Calculator at a future time when your life challenges may change. Above all, the Life Calculator empowers you to take charge of your financial future.

LifeCalculator.Net

Readers demand up-to-the-minute information and want to connect with others who have similar interests. LifeCalculator.Net is a Web site dedicated to providing a forum for the exchange of information, experiences, critiques of investment and medical products and services, as well as updates of vital governmental and tax information. The purchaser of this book will get a temporary password, register on LifeCalculator.Net and have a limited free trial period of 30 days, after which he or she will have to pay a fee in order to have continuing access to the many services, data resources, and financial calculators available on LifeCalculator.Net.

Blogging, Webcasts, and Customized Searches

LifeCalculator.Net features blogs, postings of articles from other sources, guest opinions from experts on specific financial planning matters, and e-mail exchanges among readers, guest experts, and me on personal financial planning questions. Online panels of guest experts will focus on particular topics in the book. These panels enable you to enhance your understanding of an issue that currently challenges you. The seminars are stored online and are available for you at your convenience. An issue that does not appear of interest to you today may be a crisis facing you tomorrow. You will be able to access valuable information from the Life Calculator archives instantly.

You can visit LifeCalculator.Net, as well as recommended affiliate Web sites linking to blogs. You can download posted articles and presentations, and tailor your searches to your individual needs and available time. When you access LifeCalculator.Net, whether on your PDA, cell phone, or laptop computer, you are afforded an instant, interactive experience that delivers updated information. Links to numerous retirement planning and financial investment Web sites are provided.

Personalized Bookmarks

Through the use of LifeCalculator.Net, you create a financial blueprint for your future, bookmark those sources that you will refer to for updated financial information, and develop a linked relationship to other readers who will exchange their experiences and contacts. All this data will be stored on your personal spreadsheet.

For those readers who upgrade from the basic Life Calculator to the expanded deluxe Life Calculator, continued scenario planning using information from LifeCalculator.Net is possible. You will be able to access your spreadsheet when logged onto LifeCalculator.Net, and you will revise your holdings based on updated market information, interactive discussions, retirement-oriented Web articles, and Web-available asset-allocation advisors.

Getting the Facts

Creating your financial profile, whether using the basic Life Calculator or the deluxe Life Calculator, will provide a realistic understanding of your current financial resources. You must be capable of taking actions to prevent or mitigate the impact of costly adverse events (Chapter 4). In order to gain wealth, you must be informed regarding the major dilemmas that affect your financial security: investment strategies, housing, healthcare, and insurance (Chapters 5 to 7).

Know the likely challenges of each decade ahead, and reflect on the hypothetical profiles of other individuals and families who experience life challenges and successes in order to garner valuable perspectives (Chapter 8 to 9). These chapters do not need to be read sequentially in order to contribute to your ability to execute constructive changes in your financial planning.

Ten Guiding Principles

Following are 10 things you should consider as you read this book, utilize its digital planning tools, and execute your own financial strategy:

1. *Recognize that the definition* of old age *has radically changed.* Today's 65-year-old is *middle-aged*, given the probability of living until 95.
2. *Embrace your new nonretirement—you may stay active in your career well beyond 65 and become passionately involved in community activities.* Accept the fact that you may never elect (or afford) to *retire* and instead may begin a new career or extend your current work commitment.

3. *Understand your risk tolerance and review your investment exposure on an annual basis, including your real estate assets.* Given extended longevity, it is prudent to consider making higher-risk investments and holding them into your late 50s and early 60s, if additional financial resources for retirement are still needed.

4. *Execute dynamic forecasting.* Simulations based on realistic future alternative scenarios should be the basis for setting your savings goals. Prepare for the worst-case scenario and you may be in a position to enjoy the best!

5. *Adopt a life-cycle mentality,* not the traditional straight-line financial planning approach, assuming that you will live into your 90s.

6. *Create a health balance sheet.* This should include a comprehensive statement of illnesses that you may be genetically predisposed to develop as well as those that are the most expensive or long term, including heart disease, stroke, diabetes, cancer, Alzheimer's. Healthcare costs are the tsunami of financial security with the power to wreck havoc on even the best-endowed retirement plans. Reserve against the costs of these diseases with comprehensive health and long-term care insurance and seek medical advice to defer their occurrence and limit their ravaging effects.

7. *Limit the financing of your children's college education so that your retirement savings are not at risk.* Make sure your retirement goals will be met. Then set a reasonable target for supporting college funding. The most generous gift you can give a son or daughter is your fully funded retirement—it means that they will not have to pay for caring for you. When you and your children share the burden of college expenses, they learn a crucial lesson about financial responsibility and pay a relatively low cost.

8. *Anticipate caregiver expenses* when your parents are in their 60s. Have a family discussion regarding the financial options for funding health and assisted living costs as your parents age. Secure long-term care insurance for your parents, if they

have no policy. Discuss using a reverse mortgage as a vehicle for keeping your parents in their own home. Ensure that decisions are implemented by power-of-attorney instruments, which authorize relatives to make medical and financial decisions.

9. *Exercise your mind with a 30-minute daily "jog" through LifeCalculator.Net.* Knowledge is your greatest asset. Learn about rapid changes in demographics, the world economy, innovative healthcare, and technological advances that will radically transform your future.

10. *Be proactive in planning your financial future.* A successful retirement will be yours if you are disciplined in your saving, flexible in adjusting to changing personal and economic circumstances, and positive in your outlook.

Calculating Your Odds of Disaster and Preparing for Life Changes

Owning Your Future, Reducing Risk, Making Time Your Ally, and Mastering Change—these four rules of financial security are far more than simple mantras (see Chapter 1). In order to actualize a secure financial future—which at the very minimum will provide a savings buffer to weather unexpected adverse events and might even enable many of you to earn millions—it is necessary to initiate a full analysis not only of your balance sheet, but also of your personal lifestyle. Identify those situations that are likely to derail your journey to financial economic security.

Now that many boomers are reaching 60—and recognizing that many Generation-Xers will live to 100 or, perhaps, beyond with the advances of medicine—the key is to know how to survive life's inevitable speed bumps. The Life Calculator integrates *adverse events* probabilities into a comprehensive, customized financial analysis. It measures the bank account impact of the *Dirty Dozen* adverse events.

The Dirty Dozen Adverse Events

We can roughly categorize *personal* adverse events into 10 areas:

1. Divorce
2. Job loss

3. Underfunded pension
4. Extended longevity
5. Uninsured healthcare costs
6. College expenses
7. Disability
8. Caregiving for parents
9. Nursing home and assisted living expenses
10. Unexpected family expenses

In addition to these personal adverse events, your investment portfolio could be affected by two economic variables: high inflation and volatility in market returns. In constructing your personal profile, you have discretion in deciding which and how many adverse events you wish to forecast and may chose several scenarios to measure expected potential outcomes.

Adverse Events Planning

All readers should engage in adverse events screening, as it will provide a realistic understanding of the possible risks that can threaten an otherwise solid financial plan. Your probability of experiencing at least two of the dozen events described within this chapter could be better than 50 percent. By conducting your personal analysis and integrating it with your investment decisions, you have a road map that will steer you clear of financial disaster as you seek to safely achieve your life-cycle goals.

Ranking the Financial Impact of Adverse Events

Regardless of your life-cycle stage and particular financial challenges, the Life Calculator can help you start financial planning and anticipate setbacks. What are the probabilities of these dirty dozen adverse events occurring in your life cycle? Adverse events can be grouped into three tiers, based on the expected dollar impact on your financial bottom line:

1. *Most severe impact.* Uninsured healthcare costs, underfunded pension, assisted living, loss of job, and disability will have the greatest impact on your bottom line.

2. *Severe impact.* Extended longevity beyond planned expectations, divorce, and caregiving costs; can severely affect the best financial plans.
3. *Least severe.* College tuition, unexpected family expenses, investment volatility, and higher-than-expected inflation are generally considered the least severe threats to the bottom line. However, these events, especially unplanned family expenses, could end up having a much more severe impact, if the expenses are high.

Table 4.1 shows the estimated loss a financial plan could take from any of these adverse events.

Table 4.1 Probability/Costs of Adverse Events

	Event	Odds	Loss in Wealth
Most Severe Impact	Uninsured healthcare costs	61 percent[1]	$200,000 to $300,000[2]
	Assisted living	33 percent[3]	$250,000 to $350,000[a]
	Underfunded pension	60 percent[4]	$300,000[5]
	Loss of job	12 percent[6]	$218,000 to $320,000[b,7]
	Disability	28 percent[8]	$50,000 to $300,000
Severe Impact	Longevity to 95 years	Women 33 percent[9] Men 20 percent	$300,000[10]
	Divorce	50 percent[11]	$162,750[12]
	Caregiving (elder for 10 years)	66 percent[13]	$70,000[14]
Least Severe Impact	Four years of college expenses (public and private)	35 percent[15]	$80,000/$160,000[16]
	Unexpected family expenses (annual)	34 percent	$50,000 to $300,000
	Volatility		$25,000 to $50,000
	Higher than expected inflation		$3,500 to $7,000

Notes

[a] Five years of care at either an assisted living or nursing facility

[b] Loss in wealth calculated assuming median income of $50,000, 4 months of unemployment, and reduced income of 33 to 50 percent.

Most Severe Adverse Events

Uninsured Healthcare Costs (61 Percent Odds). The number of uninsured Americans is quickly becoming an epidemic as fewer employers are offering job related healthcare insurance. (61 percent of uninsured adults had healthcare costs and 30 percent of insured paid $1,000 or more beyond premiums.)[17] Those employees who are fortunate enough to have healthcare insurance are learning that employers are capping the amount they are willing to provide in the level of benefits or requiring expensive deductibles that result in the employee assuming greater out-of-pocket expenses.

With annual healthcare premiums costing an average of $11,480 for families and $4,242[18] for individuals, many individuals and families have been confronted with the difficult choice of choosing not to insure. Failure to have healthcare insurance places an uninsured family or individual at extreme risk and threatens their ability to achieve financial security. A single uninsured healthcare incident that requires hospitalization, surgery, or extended therapy may deplete all of a person's savings and result in enormous debt. (See Figure 4.1.)

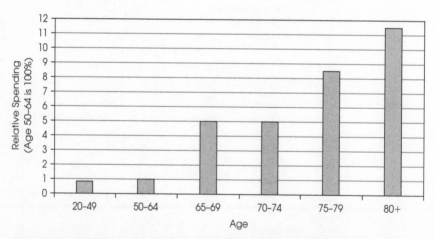

Figure 4.1   Relative Healthcare Spending by Selected Age Groups
Source: Laurence Kotlikoff and Christian Hagist, "Who's Going Broke?" NBER, Working Paper 11833 (Dec. 2005)

As you budget for retirement, you should plan for out-of-pocket medical costs of $200,000, the typical amount an otherwise-uninsured retired couple spends on Medicare premiums, prescriptions, and deductibles.[19] This figure does not include over-the-counter medications, most dental services, and long-term care. The $200,000 estimate assumes that retirees have no employer-sponsored retiree healthcare. Only one out of three employers now offers health benefits to retirees. By the time baby boomers retire, the percentage covered will likely be fewer than one in five.[20]

This $200,000 estimate is, perhaps, understated because it relies on a median life expectancy in the 80s. However, since 4 out of 10 men now 60 and more than 5 out of 10 women now 60 will live well into their 90s,[21] more realistic uninsured healthcare costs for those living longer would be nearer $300,000[22] in today's dollars. It is necessary to recognize that this 2006 figure may increase at an average annual rate of 10 percent.[23]

Continuously rising healthcare costs can quickly deplete your financial resources, including your retirement savings. This factor will need to be carefully monitored and updated in annual financial planning. Prevention of major illnesses by proper nutrition, exercise, and medical examinations will reduce your likelihood of needing expensive medical treatment.

Assisted Living and Institutional Care (33 Percent Odds). The average age of a resident in an assisted living facility in 2006 was 85, with women composing three-fourths of all residents.[24] Over one in three households,[25] given current demographic trends, will need either assisted living or nursing home care. For assisted-living facilities, not a nursing home, a private one-bedroom unit averages $32,294[26] annually with the more exclusive communities charging as much as $50,000. Factor in an expected term of residency of 2.5 years and you should plan to spend roughly $125,000 on such living arrangements.[27]

How long should you assume you might live in either assisted living or a full-service nursing care facility? Projections estimate 11 percent of 65-year-old men and almost 30 percent of women will require more than five years[28] of care in either of these two types of residences. One-third of all assisted living residents will eventually transfer to a full-service nursing facility to receive a higher level of care.[29] These nursing facilities charge an average rate for a one bedroom of $75,190 annually and $66,795 for double occupancy.[30] Assuming three years in such a nursing facility and your grand total for six years of residency in both assisted living and nursing facilities will be a whopping $325,000!

Should you be unfortunate and experience both the average unexpected healthcare costs and assisted living/nursing care costs, your budget is drained by $500,000! Fortunately, government care should cover 53 percent[31] of these total long-term-care expenses, reducing your obligation to roughly $235,000. For those who have followed my advice and secured long-term care insurance, additional savings will be achieved. (Refer to Chapter 7 for further education on health care.)

Underfunded Pension Expenses (81 Percent Odds).   Only 42 percent[32] of workers contribute to a workplace retirement-savings plan with an average balance of $58,328[33] in 401(k) accounts. Slightly less than one out of five workers working for an S&P 500 company will have a fully funded pension plan,[34] and these figures are likely to decrease as large enterprises eliminate retirement programs and small businesses fail to establish them. For middle-class workers, pensions will be only a quarter of their retirement resources, excluding housing.

If you are one of the fortunate workers with a pension program, it is essential to your financial planning that you inquire about: the portability of the pension—transferring the funds when you leave your employment; the current funding level of the pension plan and its funding for the past five years; the asset allocation mix of the plan; the percentage of the fund that is invested in your company's stock; and any restrictions on the timing of your withdrawal.

Since few employees have a fully funded pension plan and, for most, the savings amount is less than $70,000, you should not entertain illusions about the security of this source of retirement income as a potentially growing asset. To the contrary, you should assume that these funds will provide a shrinking percentage of the amount they need to cover retirement living costs.

Job Loss (12 Percent Odds).   Costs associated with job loss include both initial loss of income and the associated future wealth losses should you take a job at a lower income level, as many unemployed workers are pressured to do. The immediate job loss reduces median household wealth by an average of $20,000, although that figure is based on limited unemployment of four months[35] and a median salary of $50,000.*,[36] Obviously, that number soars over longer periods of unemployment and at higher salary levels.

Associated losses related to ongoing wealth reduction may be another one-third or one-half of your annual salary, if you are forced to take a permanent replacement job at reduced income, or if you earn significantly less than average wages. Surprisingly, 12 percent[37] of workers will be laid off or discharged each year.

For a midlife worker, job loss is far more traumatic than at an earlier age, since this is his or her peak earning period and securing a new job at the same income level is frequently difficult. As the average unemployment period extends, many workers desperately assume significantly lower paying, less challenging positions or join the growing underemployed. Only 42 percent of unemployed professionals found comparable or better work with the same pay, compared to 60 percent of Gen-Xers.[38]

This misfortune has an immediate effect on a household's finances, resulting in loss of health insurance, use of retirement nest-egg funds for living expenses, failure to continue savings plans for college expenses, and lifestyle downsizing. A conservative assumption for financial planning purposes would be four to six months without income with a replacement job income at 85 percent of previous compensation.

---

*Real median household income is $46,326

Disability (28 Percent Odds). Few readers will project a future where disability* limits their ability to work, care for themselves, and enjoy personal pursuits. Although there have been numerous references to the opportunities for successful multiphase careers, a statistically significant number of individuals will not be accorded those choices. Census data document that by the traditional retirement age of 65, 28 percent of all Americans are disabled, with 68 percent of that number being severely disabled. By age 70, that number has risen to 38 percent, with two-thirds of that number in the severe category. Only 10 years later at age 80, 72 percent of all people are disabled, 80 percent of whom are severely disabled. Nearly two out of three men (65 percent) and three out of four women (75 percent) are disabled at age 80.[39]

The effects of disability will be serious. Not only will you have to pay for any medical or caregiving expenses required by your disability, if you are not insured, but a disability during your working years will also significantly reduce your income. You can be expected to incur total disability costs of $50,000 to $300,000.

Severe Adverse Events

Living Longer than You Expected (43 to 50 Percent Odds). As Americans live longer, the gender gap for life expectancy is decreasing, with only five years difference between the expected 80 years for women and 75 years for men.[40] Although we should be thrilled that our medical progress, private healthcare system, and societal successes have enhanced and enriched our lives, giving us more time with loved ones, financial planning must be updated to recognize that an amazing one out of five men and one of three women who are 70 today will make it to their 95th birthday![41] As women are four

---

*Disability Definition: Having blindness, deafness, or severe vision or hearing impairment; having a condition that would limit one or more basic physical activities; having a physical, mental, or emotional condition longer than 6 months that would limit a person's independence, mobility, or employment activity.

times more likely than men to live to age 100, they should plan for that eventuality.[42]

Longer life expectancy is a positive—if you remain healthy and have the financial resources to live comfortably, support yourself independently, and not require financial assistance from your children and can afford the extended medical care you will require as you age. It is defined as an adverse event only because of the catastrophic costs associated with living beyond the traditional actuarial tables. Extending life an additional 15 years from 75 to 90 for a man and from 80 to 95 for a woman has substantial budgetary effects, more than doubling the costs you may have expected had you lived to merely the actuarial age.

Divorce (50 Percent Odds).   Half of all baby boomers' marriages end in divorce.[43] Following divorce, 54 percent of women[44] and 70 percent of men[45] remarry within five years. For second and third marriages, the divorce rates are even higher—for a second marriage 66 percent; for a third marriage, 73 percent.[46] At retirement, individuals who have experienced divorce have $162,750[47] less in assets than married couples. There is a decreasingly lower probability of having this adverse effect impact your balance sheet as you mature. For women, with the exception of highly paid professionals, divorce can inflict a permanent loss of financial stability; 22 percent of divorced women 65 and older lived in poverty in 2001, five times the rate of married women.[48] Proper independent financial counseling prior to a divorce can assure that taxes, child care expenses, medical arrangements, and property matters are resolved fairly.

Both single and divorced readers are advised to secure a premarital contract before marriage or remarriage that clearly defines each spouse's assets and liabilities; sharing of trust funds and estate gifts; pensions, deferred compensation, and life insurance; and future appreciation on assets acquired prior to marriage, particularly real estate. Couples may well find that running the divorce scenario through the Life Calculator will encourage them to have a frank and pragmatic discussion regarding their marriage finances, and, perhaps, those couples who are in troubled relationships may avoid taking ill-considered steps that might lead to divorce.

Caregiving (66 Percent Odds).   Millions of Americans are now joining the *Sandwich Generation* as they experience caring for their children and their parents simultaneously while planning for their own retirements. As stated before, 4 out of every 10 middle-aged households between 45 and 64 years of age will support a child under 25, as well as a parent or grandparent.[49] More than two-thirds of Americans are expected to be taking care of an elderly parent 10 years from now.[50]

The costs of this care will add to the financial burden of those preparing for retirement—additional household expenses for this care are estimated at $7,000[51] or more a year—not to mention the effects on employment. The statistics reveal the impact of caregiving on careers: 57 percent of caregivers reported to work late, left early, or had to take time off because of their responsibilities; 17 percent took a leave of absence; and 10 percent reduced their positions from full-time to part-time work.[52]

The costs will be even higher for families caring for parents suffering from dementia, as this condition often requires family caregivers to hire outside help. The previous costs apply to situations in which parents can be cared for while living in your home, but the financial parameters change dramatically when it becomes necessary for a parent to live in an assisted-living facility or nursing home.

Retiring at 65 is not likely to be a financial possibility for those of you who need steady income to provide monetary support to your extended families. Unfortunately, few families are truly prepared for this increased financial load. Many savings accounts will be quickly depleted by the costs of caring for an aging parent.

What are the odds that you will face the additional financial burden of elderly caregiving?

Depending on your age, your family's genetic history of longevity, and your parents' health, your average probability is 66 percent that you will face this financial hurdle.

These costs are enough to jolt even those with a comfortable level of financial resources into jeopardy: $200,000[53] to support a parent in assisted care for the expected duration of six years in a private one-bedroom unit. If you are married and have four living parents, you need to estimate of whether this financial exposure will be a singular event or whether there is a possibility, given your parents' health and ages, that all parents might require assisted-living support. Use the Life Calculator to determine what impact this adverse event will have on your financial security.

It is vital to follow the advice in Chapter 3:

> Anticipate caregiver expenses when your parents are in their 60s. Have a family discussion regarding the financial options for funding health and assisted-living costs as your parents age. Secure long-term care insurance for your parents, if they have no policy. Discuss using a reverse mortgage as a vehicle for keeping your parents in their own home. Ensure that decisions are implemented by power-of-attorney instruments, which authorize relatives to make medical and financial decisions.

If you realize, following such discussions with your parent(s), that you may need to supplement their funds to support their care, early action can make a substantial difference in limiting the harsh impacts that will occur to your own retirement security. Knowing when you are in your 40s or 50s the realities of elder care—and the likely amount of support your family will need to contribute—will assist you in planning options to mitigate the financial exposure.

Perhaps you will be forced to defer the traditional notion of a comfortable retirement, complete with travel and relaxation, to remain engaged in extended employment and care for loved ones. Your own retirement security may necessitate working well into your 70s. And yet the decision to extend employment past 65, often assumed to be the primary way to close the gap of limited retirement savings, will add little net value to retirement accounts, if caregiving expenses are absorbing the incremental income.

Not only will many of you find that you need to plow through your inadequate savings, but our medical and technological advances and collective prosperity means that you, too, will live longer than ever before, requiring additional financial resources to fund your extended longevity. (Refer to the discussion on longevity in this chapter.) You need to measure the cost of extended longevity in your own life and that of your family members:

1. How many elderly relatives might you need to support? Are you able to rely on sharing this responsibility with a family member?
2. What is the health of your parent(s)? Is there adequate health-care and long-term care insurance to cover most medical expenses beyond Medicaid?
3. Would you consider having your relatives live with you to assist in providing for care and reducing expenses? For further discussion, read Chapter 7 on housing.
4. Are you or will you be in a legal position to make financial and medical decisions for your parents when they are no longer independent?

Least Severe Events

College Expenses (35 Percent).[*,54]   Tuition expenses at both public and private colleges have soared. Interest rates on college loans have significantly increased in recent years. College planners now estimate a year of college at a public institution at a minimum of $20,000 with private schools topping out in the low $40,000s.[55] A major trade-off for many boomer parents who delayed having children is to decide how much funding support to provide for college while continuing to invest in their retirements.

A growing number of parents are concluding that community college education instead of a public university are preferred choices to reduce costs for the first two years of college enrollment. Living at

---

*Population age 18 to 24 enrolled in college or graduate school.

home, an ROTC scholarship, work-study arrangements, and scholarship support and financial aid should all be explored.

Unexpected Family Expenses (34 Percent).   Pew Research reported that 34 percent of Americans had unexpected expenses. These expenses may be legal, home-related, or career-related, to name a few. Are you in a business or an environment that may expose you to litigation? You may be the target of a lawsuit, and may have to pay for legal expenses or any damages against the other party.

Other events that people often do not consider are related to nature. Your home may be your largest asset, but are you failing to protect it adequately? Hurricanes, tornadoes, earthquakes, landslides, fires, and riots are just some of the disaster events that may destroy your home. Are you prepared when your 20-something son who has no health insurance is in a car accident and needs your financial support to cover legal or medical bills? Such events are a normal part of life and can cumulatively deplete your wealth. Try saving enough cash to live on for three to six months and invest it in a liquid money market account, if available. You should perform a risk analysis to determine your exposure and read carefully Chapter 7 on strategies to mitigate financial loss.

Increased Volatility.   Increased market volatility resulting in decreased returns will cause your projections of future wealth to miss their mark, exposing your family to the harmful effects of facing adverse events with limited savings, as well as the opportunity costs of higher principal and your lost compounded interest. You must constantly monitor your portfolio and protect it, especially when you are older and cannot afford erosion of principal.

Risk management is a much more critical strategy than maximizing higher return. Over a period of three years, if your projected returns were 3 percent lower than expected, you would lose $23,182 on unrealized returns on a portfolio of $250,000. If you saved $10,000 annually, that would be another $1,836 of compounded returns lost, for a total of $25,018. If your portfolio and savings rate were larger, this number will be proportionately larger—a $500,000

Table 4.2

	$250,000 Portfolio/$10,000 Annual Savings	$500,000 Portfolio/$20,000 Annual Savings
Loss if principal has 3 percent lower return	$23,182	$46,364
Loss on annual savings	$1,836	$3,672
Total	$25,018	$50,036

portfolio would lose $46,364 of unrealized returns and a savings rate of $20,000 would lose $3,672, for a total of $50,036. This is reflected in Table 4.2.

The higher the dollar value you have invested in the market, the higher the impact, as it is more difficult to earn that money back with your decreased principal. If you lose 50 percent of your principal, you have to earn back 100 percent to get back to your original level!

Higher than Expected Inflation.   Higher than expected inflation also may cripple your investment portfolio. Over the last decade, inflation has been low, so financial planners have advised using a rate of 2 to 3 percent. However, the inflation rate has historically been higher; during the 1980s, it reached double-digit levels.[56] Underestimating the inflation rate may hasten the unexpected depletion of your nest egg. For example, an inflation rate just 2 percent higher over a period of three years will add $3,525 in total unexpected costs to an annual spending of $50,000 in retirement. If your family spends double that annually, total costs would double to $7,050.

Potential Windfalls

Recent studies have indicated that few baby boomers will benefit from parental inheritances. Less than 20 percent have received an inheritance, with a median amount of $64,000.[57] Only one out of every seven anticipates collecting an inheritance.[58] Reduced inheritances are the result of parents living longer.

If you are among the 7 percent who receive more than $100,000[59] in inheritance, you have an opportunity to make up for your previous financial mistakes if you manage the inheritance prudently. If it is real estate—the family home or vacation cottage—consider appropriate strategies for selling the property and reinvesting the proceeds. Sell investments, equity, or bonds that do not add value to your diversified portfolio.

Do not view the additional windfall as monopoly money and start spending it casually. Pay down your debt, reinvest in tax-efficient investments, and limit your withdrawals—this inheritance may assist in actualizing your retirement dream.

Your Best-Case Scenario—Is It Enough?

The Number

Charting your financial course, identifying your goals, and measuring your ability to achieve financial security are all focused on a single objective: searching for the *magic number*—the sum of dollars that is expected to provide you with assured financial security and a comfortable retirement. This obsessive search for the number is misguided. As you are learning, sound financial planning must be continuously adjusted to meet the dynamics of the economic, financial, and personal changes in your life.

Expectations regarding the cost of living, level of inflation, interest-rate environment, and volatile investment returns are among the economic and financial factors that significantly affect the number. Equally important will be any adverse event that reduces your balance sheet and may limit your ability to earn income in the future.

Given the multitude of variables that may impact you as you travel through various life-cycle stages, it is more important to focus on risk management by creating alternative financial plans that can be executed than to try to identify a singular number that will become instantly outdated when any major events, external or personal, occur in your life.

Your Best-Case Scenario

Is there a best-case scenario? Absolutely! It is a financial strategy that ensures against the downside by reserving sufficient resources to off-set the more likely adverse events, while providing a platform for continuing flexibility and growth. Your best-case scenario, which you will create yourself using the Life Calculator, will be your personal reflection of the ultimate financial goals you can realistically achieve given a set of circumstances that you define. It will be your responsibility to acknowledge the economic and financial parameters that will guide your journey to the best possible outcome and to take actions to manage the risks that may occur in that journey.

Optimum Strategies for Getting from Here to There

Now that you have used the Life Calculator to create your financial profile, weighed alternative investment options, measured the impact of potential adverse events, and examined alternative scenarios, you know the power of dynamic financial planning. More important, you have taken control of your financial future. The subsequent chapters will offer valuable insights into and information about many relevant issues you need to consider: healthcare and long-term care insurance, investment options, annuities, real estate, and community and living options.

Failing to Plan . . . or Taking Responsibility for Your Future

You have just two options. Continue to assume that you will be covered or secure, thanks to whatever retirement plans you have in place (defined-benefit pensions, 401(k)s, Roth IRAs, annuities, etc.), or accept responsibility for taking a hard look at where you are financially, where you want to be in 10 or 15 or 20 years or more—and figure out how to get there. You can be sure of one thing: if you do not take on the responsibility for financial planning, odds are you will not have enough to pay for living the way you would like to live for more years than you dare to think you will live. Your failure to plan will not only affect you—it will have a severe impact on your children and grandchildren.

The Best Inheritance Is a Fully Funded Retirement

Here is the paradox: By planning strategically, you will give your heirs an inheritance they can enjoy while you are still alive; but if you don't plan, your deficit becomes their debt. Without giving them anything now, you can give them a greater inheritance later. It is, ultimately, tax-neutral. If you can pay your way, they do not have to pay for you. And that is the best inheritance you can leave in today's world.

CHAPTER 5

It's a Blur between Work and Play

As boomers extend their working years to 70 or beyond, either through necessity or personal preference, life-cycle career strategy will replace retirement planning. The hard edge between work and office will become nonexistent, as the 24-hour world overtakes the nine-to-five office structure. Readers will need to be fluid in allocating personal and business activities throughout seven-day weeks, with substantial amounts of work performed either at home or in mobile locations. Some workers will decide to transition to new careers, requiring either an expanded skills set or a professional license. Virtual learning, vocational classes, industry-sponsored seminars, or university programs will serve to prepare those seeking new opportunities.

Say Hello to Phased Careers and Delayed Retirement

Readers are advised to consciously create a multicareer strategy that recognizes the realities of a likely 50-year span of employment. Once you recover from the horror that this length of employment projects on your consciousness, you can begin building the multidecade career profile that will guide your future employment plans.

Many professions will put you in a position of needing to consider a second career. For example, some careers expect their employees to retire at 50 or 60 years of age—firefighters, teachers, or pilots, for instance. Others are employed in industries that require physical labor where working to an older age is not possible, such as mining, manufacturing, and construction. Some people are engaged by a company that is downsizing due to offshoring or business slow-downs—automotive, technology, and real estate are often impacted. Finally, some employees are simply burned out or hit a glass ceiling. Due to these factors, it is important to begin mapping new career options.

You should complete the matrix provided in the Life Calculator to correlate your education with potential employment opportunities. Importantly, overlay the matrix with information provided by the Life Calculator's Growth Industries tab for the industries and occupations expected to expand over the next two decades.

Even if you are currently employed in a comfortable position, it is important to adopt a multicareer philosophy. According to the Bureau of Labor Statistics, the average baby boomer has made 10.7 job changes in his or her career.[1] Few employees younger than 55 years of age will find that their careers are completed with one employer, while most will be required or will desire to seek new employment opportunities, including entrepreneurial enterprises. If you are anxious that your current position will not extend beyond the next five years or, if you are 55 or older and are looking at work-ing beyond 65, you should immediately initiate career planning advice to ensure that you have job opportunity choices available within the next three- to five-year horizon.

Be advised that creating a new career profile will require time to identify the new industry, target positions of interests, develop employment opportunities, and conduct job searches. The Life Cal-culator will add substantial value to your career search by providing three exercises. Two exercises measure the value of both employer-matched pension contributions and employer-provided benefits. Of great interest to all readers should be the third exercise—determining the value of working five years longer.

The Life Calculator also provides a job bank in its Growth Industries tab. Measure your future career potential by matching your current skills to those required in your selected future industry target.

What is your skills gap? Will it be necessary for you to enroll in classes to update your technology skills? Will you need to receive a particular industry certificate or degree, such as a Realtor's or RN license? Have you joined industry organizations to network among potential employers? Are you targeting Web resources related to a particular industry or career to develop knowledge of the selected job area? You should create a timeline for effecting a transition to a new industry. Realistically, such a timeline may well be multiyear, as you may determine that your next career requires significant skill or education that will need to be gained before an active job search in the new industry or occupation can begin.

Such conscious multitiered life career planning will prepare you for the realities of a rapidly changing global job market where once-dominant industries have become outdated by new technologies and where skills once valued have lost market importance. As you create a life career plan, consider what actions are required to ensure that you develop the new skills and industry knowledge needed to smoothly move to a new job environment, when desired or when necessitated by a job loss.

Working to 70 and Beyond

Thirty years ago, the stereotypical 65-year-old employee retired from full-time work and moved to a resort retirement community in Arizona, Florida, or California. Increased longevity, inadequate resources for retirement, changing economic factors such as health-care costs, and different attitudes toward work are keeping people at their jobs well beyond the typical retirement age.

A 2006 AARP study reported that by 2012, nearly 20 percent of the U.S. workforce will be 55 or older, up from 14 percent in 2002. About 40 percent of AARP members over 50 either are working or plan to work past age 65.[2]

Today, more than one out of three Americans will live past 90, having more opportunities in their life for multiple careers.[3] *Retirement* is becoming phased—no longer a sharp end to a career, but rather a turning point in a journey that may move forward to other employment opportunities.

According to a 2005 AARP survey of baby boomers aged 50 to 65, two out of three workers are interested in such a gradual, phased retirement. *Rehirement* and *preretirement* serve as buzzwords that describe the third stage of life in which a work-life balance that achieves your financial needs also leaves you time to attend to your hobbies. Depending on your economic needs, health, and personal passions, you may never formally "retire" from the workforce.

Many generational icons have remained intellectually and physically able past the stereotypical retirement age: Alan Greenspan (formerly Federal Reserve chairman) was 79 years old when he retired; Kirk Kerkorian (president/CEO of Tracinda Corporation) is investing globally at 90; Warren Buffet (chairman of Berkshire Hathaway) is still active at 77; and Rupert Murdoch (owner of News Corporation) is expanding his media empire at 76. Rod Stewart at 62, Mick Jagger at 64, and Barbara Streisand at 65,* continue to perform to sold-out audiences, all examples that many of today's 60-year-olds have the energy, health, and professional focus of the previous generation's 45-year-olds—confirming the belief that age 60 is now middle age, given the longevity cycle for many people to live beyond 90.

Most families will find that they cannot fund a potential 30 years of retirement—to age 95—with 40 years of work. When Social Security was created and current defined-benefit plans initiated, individuals who retired at 65 could be expected to live less than 10 years past their retirement date. Their 40 years of work supported a less than 10-year retirement period, on average. For the one out of five men and one out of three women currently in their 60s expected to live to 95, it will be difficult to live comfortably on retirement income that begins at age 65.

---

*All as of September 1, 2007.

Early retirement is even more financially challenging with the disincentive of decreased Social Security benefits. According to the Social Security Administration, depending on age, people taking early retirement at age 62 could receive a 20 percent reduction in benefits[4] for the rest of their life, but for every year they retire later than 65, their benefits could increase by 8 percent until age 70.[5] Using the Life Calculator, you are able to determine the financial gain from working an additional five years to age 70. (See Table 5.1.)

Table 5.1   Approximate Annual Social Security Benefit by Retirement Age and Annual Income Level[a]

	Retirement Age		
Annual Earnings	62	66	70
$20,000	$6,816	$9,480	$12,888
$30,000	$8,436	$11,844	$16,224
$40,000	$10,080	$14,208	$19,548
$50,000	$11,700	$16,560	$22,872
$60,000	$13,344	$18,936	$26,208
$70,000	$14,952	$20,928	$28,200
$80,000	$15,972	$22,068	$29,760
$90,000	$16,740	$23,148	$31,320
$100,000	$17,496	$24,204	$32,748
$110,000	$18,156	$24,996	$33,684
$120,000	$18,648	$25,584	$34,332
$130,000	$19,008	$26,040	$34,860
$140,000	$19,236	$26,340	$35,196
$150,000	$19,320	$26,460	$35,340
$160,000	$19,320	$26,460	$35,352
$170,000	$19,320	$26,460	$35,352
$180,000	$19,320	$26,460	$35,352
$190,000	$19,320	$26,460	$35,352
$200,000	$19,320	$26,460	$35,352
$250,000	$19,320	$26,460	$35,352

Note:
[a]Calculated using the Social Security Quick Calculator at: www.ssa.gov/OACT/quickcalc/index.html. Assumes person born 1/1/1946 and the assumptions of the Quick Calculator.

If you decide to delay retirement, you will find that you are in the majority. According to a 2006 Conference Board Survey, over half of baby boomers say they wish to continue working. Three out of four respondents say that they lacked sufficient funds to retire, and two out of five respondents report that they need to keep working for the medical benefits.[6] The economic return from working one to five years past retirement is substantial, adding 9 to 56 percent more annual retirement income for the average household, depending on whether retirement is delayed one or five years.[7]

Although more than 70 percent of baby boomers plan to keep working past age 65, only about a quarter of employers have plans under way to employ them.[8]

The goal of a new career may well be to work enough hours to pay the bills and to prevent drawing down on your retirement. Take advantage of your employer's health and 401(k) plans, as they are pretax opportunities to save additional money. If working on your own, purchase health and long-term care insurance, as these premiums are deductible as a business expense, if you establish a home office.

Life Calculator Exercise SEVEN: Working Longer

Analyze the benefits of working five years beyond your traditional retirement age of 65. Log on to www.LifeCalculator.Net and follow the Working Longer Exercise link to find out!

Targeting Growth Industries

Over the next 10 years, as retirements increase in traditional baby boomer–dominated industries, numerous opportunities will appear for those willing to relocate or take the time to learn new skills.

Important industry sectors can be roughly classified into three categories:

1. High-growth areas include education, healthcare, trade, leisure and hospitality, and professional and business services. Job growth in the services sector will account for three-quarters of all new jobs.
2. Net growth areas include information technologies, finance, transportation, construction, utilities, and the public sector.
3. Declining industries include manufacturing, agriculture, forestry, fishing, hunting and mining.

In looking at Figure 5.1, you are advised to concentrate your second career job searches in areas of expected employment growth.

Several trends are making it easier for midcareer workers to transition to another industry, despite the increased probability of age

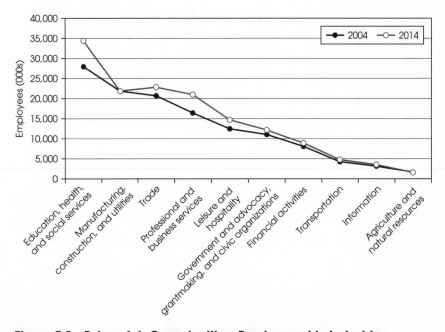

Figure 5.1   Future Job Opportunities: Employment in Industries Covered in the Bureau of Labor Statistics Career Guide

Source: Bureau of Labor Statistics, "Career Guide to Industries, Overview and Outlook," www.bls.gov/oco/cg/indchar.htm

bias. Many of the new jobs in the service sector are knowledge and information based, valuing career experiences and not limited by physical restrictions. Although some of the early-stage baby boomers will be retiring, others will be seeking second or third careers. Employers, seeking to replace their more experienced workers, may find more mature employees attractive.

You must be proactive when attempting to switch careers in midlife or to reenter the job market if currently unemployed. Successful job candidates will have prepared themselves by taking university-based programs to update their skills. They will attend targeted industry events to gain industry perspective and to develop industry contacts, and will have updated their resume and cover letter to send perspective employers.

To be competitive, a successful job candidate should:

- Identify the growth industry of interest.
- Decide if the pay level and benefits, especially health, pension and/or employer-matched savings are sufficient to meet needs.
- Check the geographic limitations and the schedule flexibility; determine whether full-time, part-time, and teleworking is possible.
- Determine the education or skill set that is needed to be a competitive job candidate in that industry.

Recognize that such career planning efforts, while demanding a commitment of time that might otherwise be spent for personal or family activities, will be richly rewarded in future years when you experience burnout, find that you are likely to be pink-slipped, hit a proverbial glass ceiling, or face pressures to retire from your current job.

What Industry Sectors Show Promising Job Growth?

Healthcare and business services including technology, leisure, and hospitality are the four industry sectors expected to grow faster than average over the next 15 years. In addition, the exodus of the baby-boom generation will generate a substantial number of skilled job openings. Even assuming that some of the baby boomers defer retirement, additional job opportunities will exist in the following occupations:[9]

- Health
  - Registered nurses
  - Nursing aides and orderlies
  - Home health aides
  - Medical assistants
  - Personal and home care aides
- Education
  - Postsecondary teachers
  - K–12 school teachers
  - Education administrators, K–12
- Technology
  - Computer support specialists
  - Computer software engineers
  - Computer systems analysts
  - Network systems and data communications analysts
  - Network and computer systems administrators
- Customer Services
  - Waiters and waitresses
  - Taxi drivers and chauffeurs
  - Retail salespersons
  - Customer service representatives
- Public Services
  - Firefighters
  - EMTs and paramedics
  - Hazardous material removal workers
- Professional Positions
  - General and operations managers
  - Accountants and auditors
  - Employment recruiting specialists
  - Airline pilots, copilots, flight engineers
- Trade
  - Carpenters

- Science
  - Medical/clinical lab technicians
  - Medical scientists

Many of these occupations are crucial components to industries projected to grow the fastest over the next decade. For older workers in these skill categories, the chance of finding employment is very high.

Benefit-Rich Industries

Learning to perform a valuation of benefit-rich industries is just as important as selecting growth industries and skill sets that are likely to continue to offer value. The Life Calculator is unique in its ability to assist readers in measuring the financial value of employer-provided benefits, including pensions and healthcare, in an age in which increasing numbers of employers have restructured their benefit packages to substantially reduce their retirement and healthcare contributions. Weighing as significantly as the issue of salary or hourly wage are the values derived from tax-free retirement and health benefits. When seeking employment opportunities, you should acknowledge the long-term economic impact of such benefits.

A major reason why workers seek to continue in positions that are otherwise unattractive or why older workers choose to work longer is the opportunity to preserve benefits packages. Such benefits can provide an employee with employer-supported healthcare, employer contributions for pensions, paid leave for family care, and career education.

These benefit packages save employees tens of thousands of dollars a year in premiums alone that they would have to fund, if employed in other job environments that did not provide similar benefits. They also provide additional years of long-term financial security through employer match or direct defined-benefit programs, and they create job flexibility that permits care for children, disabled family, and aging parents. These benefits provide a significant financial incentive to either continue at your current

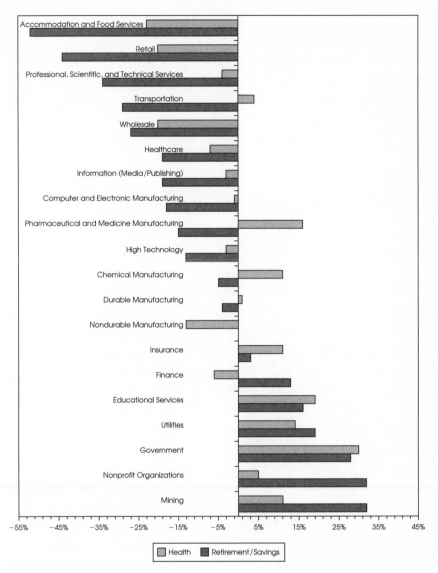

Figure 5.2   Employee Benefits by Industry (Difference from Market Median)

Source: Mercer Human Resource Consulting, "2005 Spotlight on Benefits Report," www.mercerhr.com/pressrelease/details.

job or to identify another employer with equal or greater benefits.[10] As Figure 5.2 projects, those industries with both positive health and retirement benefits greater than the median include insurance, educational services, utilities, government, nonprofit organizations, and mining. All but mining are growth industries and should be the target of your second-career job search.

Given the economic value that such benefits represent, readers should prioritize the availability of such benefits when considering job opportunities. Two examples that confirm the long-term value of such benefits are discussed next.

If you were to save $5,000 a year in a 401(k) that returned 5 percent annually, you would have $113,287 in your 401(k) at the end of 15 years. If your employer contributed $1,000 annually, you would have earned $135,945 at the end of 15 years, a difference of 20 percent.

Compare the benefit of having an employer-supported healthcare plan. For example, a conventional healthcare plan for a single person with employer support on average costs $3,780 in premium costs annually in 2005; you would probably pay $500 and your employer would pay $3,280.[11] Your savings would total $74,317, if the $3,280 were compounded at 5 percent over 15 years. Determine you own health savings using the Life Calculator.

Flexible Careers

Information technology—for example, the computer, the Internet, mobile phones, and teleconferencing—has drastically changed the working environment. As a result of the Information Revolution, people can work globally from anywhere. Entrepreneurial businesses and telecommuting are just two areas of opportunity that technology has transformed.

The fusion of technology and employment is best expressed in virtual education and phased careers. Today's online and distance learning allow education that is unlimited by geographic region and available to all. This virtual education becomes necessary if you are to garner the knowledge and skills necessary to work, or if you want to pursue another career in your later life. Many people are phasing into second and even third careers.

If you were to lose your job, rather than seeking a new corporate position, you might seek a more entrepreneurial route. In the 55 to 64 age group, self-employment is the fastest-growing career choice,[12] proving that age-associated experience and connections are a positive contributor to business.[13] Entrepreneurs value the greater flexibility in hours, the opportunity to set their own financial goals, and the financial rewards that may come from their hard work.

> The proportion of self-employed workers rises with age, peaking at 20 percent for women at age 66 and 38 percent men at age 65.[14]

If self-employment is not your passion, perhaps selecting an employer who is open to telecommuting will provide much of the same job flexibility. In a 2005 survey of more than 1,000 large employers, two out of five (44 percent) U.S companies reported that some of their employees telecommuted, up from one out of three (31 percent) in 2001.[15] Telecommuting is becoming increasingly accepted in the work world. Deloitte & Touche recently predicted that by 2008, 1 out of 4 U.S. employees will telework one day a week and 1 in 10 will be telework from home at least one day a month.[16]

According to a Hudson Productivity Survey, telecommuting is popular (see Figure 5.3). Nearly 6 out of 10 workers want to telework at least part time.[17] However, you should remember that telecommuting may have its negatives. For the midlevel employee who desires a management position or promotion but is not in the office to be observed or to practice management skills, telecommuting may not be the best choice. Forty-three percent of executives report that tele-commuting was best for staff-level employees, 18 percent responded that managers benefited from its use, and 66 percent answered that senior executives never or rarely telecommute.[18]

The prevalence of telecommuting varies by industry. A 2005 Bureau of Labor Statistics study ranked the following professions by their level of teleworking:[19]

1. Management, business, and financial operations (30.6 percent)
2. Professional (28.1 percent) including:
   a. People in the education, training and library fields (49.3 percent)
   b. Lawyers (44.8 percent)
   c. Managers (39.4 percent)
3. Services (11.5 percent)
4. Sales (19.8 percent)
5. Office and administrative support (9.4 percent)

As Figure 5.3 indicates, almost 60 percent of employees report that they would be comfortable working at least part-time at home, as their ideal workplace situation.

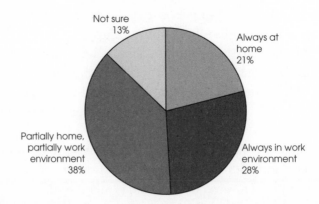

Figure 5.3   Response to "What Would be Your Ideal Workplace Situation?"

Source: "Home and Office—Workers Want It All," Hudson Productivity Survey (July 19, 2006).

Enhancing Your Skills

Not only has technology changed the business environment, but it has changed the way you will learn. The Internet enables online and distance learning, assisting thousands of U.S. workers with the knowledge and skills to stay competitive. Online education may advantage you by allowing you to have a flexible schedule for your work or family obligations, self-pace your learning schedule for optimum results, and offer course credit for previous job experience.

You may decide to go back to school in order to:

- Receive a higher salary, advance, or change your career. Almost 40 percent of online degree seekers are adults expecting to acquire new credentials in search of a better job or new career.[20]
- Follow your interests. Many online degree seekers take classes to indulge hobbies or begin courses related to interests in a new field.

Will employers recognize an online degree or a certificate? In a 2005 survey of 500 companies, 60 percent of employers said that online instruction was equally or more valuable than face-to-face instruction, with less than 10 percent commenting that it was less valuable.[21] Online degrees in subjects such as business, information technology, and health appear to meet the least resistance. They are even more accepted if they are from known "brand" schools.[22]

6

Home Is More than the Place You Live

Your home is your castle becomes an apt phrase to define the role of housing, as it becomes increasingly the center of both your business and personal world, with more and more people choosing to work from home. Communal housing developments, multigenerational housing, foreign domiciles, and assisted care will be living options on your horizon. Many readers will transition from one form of housing to another as they age.

As longevity increases and people work into their 70s and live into their 90s, lifestyle decisions will take on greater importance. No longer are people choosing to move at the traditional retirement age of 65 to retirement destinations, as many remain committed to career opportunities.

If people are telecommuting, they may elect to move to locales where taxes and living expenses are less onerous. A globally connected world may make retiring abroad a more attractive decision for those seeking lower-cost environments with a dash of native culture.

Too Much Housing—A Risky Bet?

For most readers, housing represents the largest asset in their portfolio, averaging 40 percent of their net worth.[1] Throughout the years 2000 to 2005, housing was viewed as a sure-win asset that, even after paying broker commission fees, property taxes, and, for high-valued properties, a capital gains tax, was an asset that generated attractive double-digit annual returns. The appreciated value of homes in recent years has led many families to stretch their finances, purchasing bigger homes in better locations with the objective of securing even higher net profits upon the sale of their properties.

Even before the housing slowdown at the end of 2005—a phenomena that most savvy economists and real-estate gurus anticipated—readers should have been advised to consider a fundamental question: Is housing too overweighted in my portfolio? Despite the hype of the real estate community and the buzz at backyard barbecue parties that any house purchase would lead to an instant lottery win, economic analysis proves otherwise. Yes, you can have too much housing in your portfolio! This conclusion is best understood by examining the Blackberrys, one of the 10 hypothetical profiles discussed in this book.

The Blackberrys, a professional couple both recently terminated from Enron, had identified job opportunities in Austin, Texas, the state's capital and, importantly, a less inflated housing market than Houston, where their Enron jobs had been located. The ripple effect of the Enron meltdown was clearly being reflected in the Houston real estate market where, unfortunately, the Blackberrys faced an oversupply of homes when they decided to sell their residence. Despite the almost 10 percent loss in expected value of their home due to the decision of many of their neighbors to also sell, the Blackberrys were able to derive $700,000 in net proceeds after paying off their mortgage from their home sale, after paying a 25 percent capital gains tax on the amount above the first $500,000. and the standard 6 percent in broker commission and fees.

The Blackberrys had heard from their friends about the latest popular retirement savings strategy—buying a larger home with the objective of appreciated returns. Visiting many open houses in Austin, the Blackberrys were excited by the lower home values and the diversity of inventory. They realized, prior to buying a house, that they needed to make a fundamental decision: Should they play the housing speculation game by buying a more expensive $1 million home, investing $500,000 of their $700,000 home sale profit in a down payment, or should they purchase a smaller town-house priced at $450,000, investing $200,000 as a down payment? This is an easy investment comparison, if you use the Life Calculator Housing Module, which will automatically perform a personal break-even analysis. A quick review of the investment issues is presented in Table 6.1.

Table 6.1   Investment Alternatives: Large Home versus Smaller Home

	Larger Home ($1,000,000)	Smaller Home ($450,000)	Invested Difference
Down payment	$500,000	$200,000	$300,000
Monthly mortgage[a]	$4,219	$2,110	$2,109
Available employer match	$0	$10,000	$10,000
Annual maintenance cost	$30,000	$13,500	$16,500
Home appreciation[b]	**$1,933,400**	**$870,030**	
Return on $300,000 invested at 6 percent for 15 years		**$718,967**	
Return on monthly mortgage difference compounded over 15 years at 6 percent		**$547,150**	
Difference in taxes and annual maintenance costs of large versus small home ($16,500) over 15 years at 6 percent		**$337,540**	
Employer match return ($10,000 over 15 years at 6%)		**$222,760**	
Wealth at end of 15 years	**$1,933,400**	**$2,696,450**	$763,040

Notes:
[a] Ken Blackberry, at 60 years of age, is planning to retire in 10 years, so the Blackberrys decide to assume a 15-year mortgage.
[b] 6 percent a year for 15 years. The Blackberrys did not make enough to be taxed capital gains but will pay a 6 percent commission fee when selling.

Let's analyze the Blackberrys' home-purchase options. Adding in the returns from the difference in down payment invested ($718,967), monthly mortgage payments invested ($547,150), taxes and maintenance costs invested ($337,540), and employer match ($222,760) to the appreciation of a smaller home, the Blackberrys conclude that the purchase of the smaller home will provide an additional $763,040 at the end of 15 years, the difference between $2,676,450 and $1,933,400. The investment gain from buying the smaller house translates into 19 years of additional retirement security, assuming the Blackberrys draw down $40,000 a year to supplement Social Security and pensions.

The Blackberrys learned a lesson from their Enron careers that appearance does not translate into financial security. After using the Life Calculator and seeing the superior investment results, the Blackberrys opt for a smaller home, trading off a less glamorous lifestyle for greater security in their retirement years.

Buying a larger home is a definite lifestyle choice. If you wish to have a large home, you must be willing to pay the price and recognize that it might not result in the highest return on your investment dollars. Using the Life Calculator, you will evaluate the trade-offs between lifestyle and future financial security.

Timing the Market: Cashing Out at the Peak

Strapped for cash? Desperate for a way to catch up on retirement savings or to recover from damage in your investment portfolio? Planning to downsize your home as your children depart the nest? The decision as to when to sell an appreciated home is the most important economic decision that readers will make.

For many readers, your home has been your most successful investment. Over the past 15 years, average home appreciation has reached almost 130 percent, with Pacific and Mountain states exceeding over 160 percent appreciation. Central parts of the United States experienced less than 100 percent appreciation over the same time period.[2] Impressive as that it, that level of appreciation was not competitive with the 281 percent return of the Dow Jones or the

367 percent return of the S&P 500 over the same time period. Nevertheless, most homeowners viewed their housing appreciation as central to their retirement goals. Importantly, over the last 10-year period from 1996 through 2006, housing appreciation on average equaled 103 percent, outperforming the 99 percent Dow Jones return, yet lagging the 136 percent S&P 500 return during the same time period.*

Only over the last five years, from 2001 to 2006, housing actually outperformed both market indicators, appreciating 57 percent compared to the 12.5 percent appreciation in the Dow and the 21.5 percent uptick in the S&P 500. Hence, the timing of the purchase and sale of one's home dramatically affects its net asset value, as illustrated in Table 6.2.

Readers should become informed regarding their local real estate market cycles in anticipation of their desire to eventually sell their home. It may well be necessary to sell your primary residence prior to your ideal retirement period, if you are to capture the advantage of a peak in housing prices. The Life Calculator is able to provide a comparative evaluation of the net advantage of selling a home at peak value and renting for a period of years versus delaying a sale until one is ready to repurchase a home or relocate elsewhere.

For instance, readers who intended to sell their primary residence by 2008 and capture its peak value should have sold their property in the first half of 2005, when property values peaked in most markets. Smart readers would have been able to anticipate that real estate markets were reaching a peak by reviewing the various sources listed in the Investment tab of the Life Calculator. The 2005 transition from a seller's market to a buyer's market will take its toll on any reader who is compelled to sell a home in the next few years, when the real estate market is expected to remain in a cyclical downturn.

---

*All Dow Jones and S&P dividend adjusted returns calculated by author, over the same time period as the housing report, period ending March 31, 2006.

Table 6.2 Effect of Timing on Investments

Percent Change in Prices[a]		S&P500 (TR)	Dow Jones (PR)	All U.S	Pacific States	Mountain States
1 Year	Since 2005	11.7	5.8	12.5	18.0	17.8
5 Year	Since 2001	21.5	12.5	57.3	95.6	54.8
10 Year	Since 1996	135.7	98.8	103.0	169.5	98.3
15 Year	Since 1991	367.3	281.3	129.3	162.2	176.0
26 Year	Since 1980	2624.8	1313.8	293.8	474.9	262.2

Percent Change in Prices	S. Atlantic States	Mid-Atlantic States	New England States	East South Central States	West South Central States	West North Central States	East North Central States
1 Year	17.2	13.3	8.7	7.7	7.7	6.2	5.6
5 Year	69.3	71.4	66.3	26.0	26.2	36.3	28.6
10 Year	113.4	111.7	135.5	54.7	56.5	79.4	65.0
15 Year	140.1	123.8	134.4	91.5	85.4	120.5	107.0
26 Year	308.0	419.3	527.9	172.4	113.3	197.4	216.4

Note:

[a] Period Ended March 31, 2006

Table 6.3 Effect of Housing Downturn on Asset Value

Home value	$650,000
Sale price: 15% below market	$552,500
Loss	$97,500
Loss compounded over 15 years[a]	$202,696
Years lost retirement security[b]	4

Notes:

[a] 5 percent return

[b] Assuming the average middle-class two-income family earning $150,000 a year withdrew $50,000 a year in savings during retirement to supplement their Social Security payment of $45,000.

What is the potential impact on your overall financial security of netting 15 percent less in the value of your home? If your housing asset represents more than 40 percent of your overall portfolio, that loss of value will cost you several years of retirement security, as reflected in Table 6.3.

No other asset in your portfolio will have such a substantial weight—positive or negative—on your personal wealth. Residential housing, unlike any other asset in your portfolio, is laden with emotional issues. Status, family memories, community relationships, and lifestyle comforts are all interwoven with the most strategic decision of your investment portfolio: a willingness to sell your housing asset in an appreciated market.

If you choose to remain in your home beyond its maximum value, you are placing an implicit dollar value on your personal happiness and are willing to trade future financial security for the enjoyment of additional years in your home. That decision should be consciously and carefully weighed, as the impact on your future financial options is irreversible.

Sometimes It Pays to Be a Renter in a Mobile Society

Readers will want to review the section "Too Much Housing—A Risky Bet?" because much of the same economic analysis drives the decision on renting versus buying. However, this analysis is extremely sensitive to local market variables. Certain markets throughout the country have historically expensive rents—New York City, San Francisco and Los Angeles—while others are viewed as bargains.[3] Perhaps the most important factor for consideration in the rent-versus-buy analysis is the length of time that you intend to spend in your new residence.

If you are contemplating tenancy of less than seven years, then renting is clearly the obvious choice, due to high ownership costs such as mortgage fees, mortgage interest, commissions, taxes, and insurance that cannot be fully amortized over a shorter appreciation period. Consider these six questions when evaluating whether to rent or buy:

1. Are you in an appreciating housing market cycle? If the answer is yes and you determine that you are at the beginning of the housing cycle with prices continuing to rise for five to seven years, you would be motivated to buy.
2. Do you intend to remain in your property for seven years or longer? If so, buying is a good financial decision.
3. Compare tax-advantaged investments such as municipal bonds or TIPS to your tax savings as a homeowner. Which is the better bargain?
4. Will your home purchase require you to place more than 40 percent of your assets into housing? If so, you should buy a less-expensive home.
5. If quality schools are important, are you better off renting in a more expensive community than buying in a less expensive area with poorer schools?
6. Is your employment secure? Layoffs and job transfers would necessitate a premature sale of property, possibly at a loss.

In using the Life Calculator's Rent versus Buy Model, several factors will influence your decision to buy or rent (see Table 6.4):

- The smaller the difference between your rent and your monthly mortgage payment, the higher the likelihood that you will be encouraged to buy versus rent.

Table 6.4   Renting versus Owning

	$400,000 Home[a]	Rent	Difference Placed in Investments[b]
Monthly costs	Rent $1,798[c] Costs: $1,666	$2,000[d]	$1,464
Down payment	$100,000	$0	$100,000

Renting is better than owning after 14 years if you place the down payment and difference in monthly costs into a more diversified portfolio.

Notes:
[a] Home appreciates at 6 percent annually.
[b] Difference between homeowner costs and renting. Investment return 5 percent and capital gains tax of 25 percent.
[c] 30-year mortgage is 6 percent. Annual taxes and maintenance fees are 5 percent. You will pay a commission of 6 percent when you sell you house.
[d] Rent increases at 3 percent annually.

- If house appreciation rates are lower than investment returns, you will be advised to rent.
- Your willingness to take on a longer-term mortgage, lowering monthly payments and extending your amortization of closing costs over a longer period, increases the attraction of buying versus renting.

How many years is it financially attractive for you to rent? In this scenario, the Life Calculator figures that it will take fourteen years before your home appreciation exceeds the return you can achieve from investing your rent savings. You would be advised not to purchase, if you are not going to remain in the home past fourteen years.

New Kind of Commune: This Time You Want to Belong

Many baby boomers grew up visiting their grandparents in retirement communities and recall vividly the massive leisure world cities populated by golf carts, hectic with tightly scheduled activities, and seemingly endless rows of nearly identical attached housing units.

Bridge clubs, aerobics classes, political debates, sculpture studios, and occasional guest chefs were the menu of an active retirement community where all white, higher-income members "worked" their retirement dreams.

Today's adult communities reflect a broader range of residents and lifestyles. Ten years ago, most residents in adult communities would be fully retired. Today, 45 percent to 60 percent are still working, according to surveys at Robson Communities and Pulte Homes, two of the country's largest builders of 55-or-older retirement communities.[4] Many activities now meet on evenings and weekends to ensure the participation of working residents. Community facilities now include conference rooms and business offices that can be scheduled by residents for their work activities.

Beyond these traditional adult communities, planned and developed by major builders, is a new housing option: *cohousing.* Small, self-planned communal housing projects designed as cooperative housing developments are springing up throughout the country. Those seeking a sense of community may be attracted to a supportive environment that brings together people with similar backgrounds. Today, 80 intergenerational cohousing communities house 5,000 people in the United States, and about 100 more communities are being planned.[5]

These communities feature independent housing units with common areas for guest apartments, hospitality areas, and medical suites or visits by residents' personal doctors. This style of housing requires participation in the creation and management of the community, but its smaller size and sense of closeness with friends may make it attractive.

Those contemplating creating a cooperative housing venture should be flexible in location, as this newer concept is still in its infancy. Given that the planning process in many communities takes two to three (or more) years from beginning of planning to occupancy by its residents, more traditional builders are beginning to show interest in this new market opportunity, creating their own brand of hybrid cooperative housing projects.

Extending from the objective of cooperative housing's shared community is a new version, termed *pack retirement*, in which those who already know each other chose to create a shared community. The benefits of such arrangements go beyond economics when you consider the strong social networks built, which can contribute to health during retirement.

Finally, a new and promising option is the *virtual retirement community*. For those already comfortable in their community and who wish to remain in their own homes, it is still possible to create a sense of community and a communal-style housing arrangement by forming associations, agreeing to share among members a set of services. A group of residents forms an association that provides services to support members between the ages of 50 and 90, enabling them to remain in place. Such services, for which members pay $500 to $750 a year, with some members receiving subsidies, include weekly grocery shopping, repair referrals, transportation to medical appointments, and exercise programs. Working with neighborhood businesses, members often receive these services at a 10 to 50 percent discount.[6] Those interested in forming their own virtual retirement communities can purchase a manual, complete with advice, a business plan, and marketing materials.[7]

Assisted Living: What's Likely to Happen?

The term *assisted living* raises the specter of large institutional facilities occupied by infirm and elderly residents unable to care for themselves. This commonly held image does not accurately reflect the diversity of assisted-living arrangements, which now can include at-home care. One out of three[8] readers will find themselves living in an assisted-living facility or nursing home.*,[9] The Life Calculator provides the tool for readers to review the economic impact of assisted living on their personal wealth.

---

*11 percent of 65-year-old men and almost 30 percent of women will require more than five years of care.

Assisted-living varies from a scale of a few residents to several hundred apartments, offering alternative living options from shared rooms, deluxe suites, or independent apartment units. Many assisted-living facilities provide 24-hour on-call assistance, meal services, social activities, and personal care and medication management, where needed, for its residents. Assisted-living expenses must be paid out of pocket, as Medicare and Medicaid pay little of the costs.

Continuing-care facilities, a form of assisted living, allow residents a continuum of care within a community, allowing them to graduate from fully independent living to units where medical care and daily services are provided. All these facilities require a substantial entrance fee that may be partly refunded and monthly fees ranging from $1,000 to $10,000.[10]

Recently there have been new developments in assisted living. Seniors who need the services of assisted living, but who insist on living at home, may elect to have the services come to them. Caregivers, many of whom are affiliated with assisted-living campuses or developments, will provide daily support for their clients, integrating them into the activities of their affiliated nearby facilities.

Such at-home care is not inexpensive. Although long-term care insurance may pay a portion of the daily fees, which can total $150 to $300 daily, comparable in costs to living in the facilities themselves, which generally range from $4,000 to $8,000 a month. For those who need to eventually transition to an assisted-care or nursing facility, at-home care can afford clients priority on the waiting list of the facility where their caregiver services are affiliated.

Selecting an assisted-living facility requires care and planning. It is best approached far in advance of when the decision to move is needed. Make certain that you are clear regarding the return of the entrance fees, if you chose to move upon your spouse's death, or if you may require a more intensive nursing-care environment. Verify the basis on which monthly fees are charged: Are they all-inclusive, or are there additional charges beyond the fee? Finally, how frequently will the fees increase? Consult your lawyer and accoutant before making any decisions.

Bringing Your Parents Home

The most difficult transition for families is to reverse the role of parenting. Yet, it is a task that will occur with increasing frequency as Baby Boomers age and longevity increases well beyond 90 years. Currently, 17 percent of households in the United States care for at least one person age 50 or older.[11] Ten years from now, more than two-thirds of baby boomers are expected to be taking care of an elderly parent.[12]

You may be faced with the tough decision of whether to bring your parents home. For some families, the decision is financial—they simply have run out of money to pay for nursing facilities and do not wish to have their parents living in a poorer-quality nursing home on Medicaid, sharing a room and receiving care from strangers.

Other families are simply respecting their parents' or relatives' desire not to be institutionalized, preferring to provide care at home. Sometimes it may be possible to provide distance caregiving. An estimated 5 million Americans manage the care of elderly relatives from a distance, living an hour or more away from their relative.[13] The average caregiver was 51 years old, 450 miles away, a relative, and spent $400 a month on travel and other costs related to care.[14]

Three major considerations loom in making this important decision in how to care for your parent or relative:

1. Managing the care
2. Providing attractive, safe, and private accommodations
3. Financing the costs of the care and any needed home alterations

Managing the care of your family member entails hiring a personal assistant to care for your parent or relative, helping with bathing, dressing, meals, activities, and transporting your loved one to medical appointments. If you are working, such an assistant may be needed for as many as 11 hours a day during the week and limited occasions on weekends.

Families who have a spare bedroom can utilize that area. However, it may need to be enlarged to provide adequate space for medical equipment and to create a sitting room environment, as well as bedroom and bathroom facilities. Lighting, color, height of counters, and surface of floors are important considerations for comfort and safety.

If an available room does not exist, families may consider adding a room, creating an efficiency apartment with large amounts of light and handicap access, which they could expect to spend a one-time $50,000 to $75,000 to build. Such costs certainly seem reasonable, with annual $71,000 plus budgets for a nursing home.

Many married couples may well be faced with the care of multiple aging parents. Under those conditions, it is probably not feasible to consider at-home care, unless the purchase of a larger family home is possible to accommodate the care of your parents. Please read carefully the discussion in Chapter 4 regarding caregiving and then utilize the Life Calculator to measure the financial impact that caregiving obligations will have on your own balance sheet.

Financing in-home care is a patchwork quilt, requiring you to draw on your parents' or relatives' pension, Social Security, Medicaid, long-term care insurance, and, in some cases, reverse-mortgage payments. More affluent families may supplement their parents' financial resources and benefit from the cash deduction of taking an elderly parent or relative as a dependent. States have become increasing flexible in allowing Medicaid money to pay for assisted-living care at home, with 49 states allowing such waivers. However, utilizing Medicaid funds imposes a limited number of hours of care a day and restricts choice of providers from an approved list.

Your Home Can Stay in the Family

You are living in a home that you love and would hope to stay in as long as your heath permits. Your home is also your major asset and will be the most valuable component of your estate. How do you protect your estate from paying exorbitant taxes on your home, which is likely to appreciate significantly in value over your lifetime? Is it possible for you to use your home as an income stream in your retirement to further expand your financial resources?

With astute estate planning and the willingness to educate yourself to the pros and cons of a qualified personal residence trust (QPRT) that shelters your home from living estate taxes, you may be able to both live in your home and later transfer it to your heirs with favorable tax treatment. If you question your ability to afford living in your home, a reverse mortgage can translate your home's value into a cash stream.

Although it is uncertain what action Congress will take regarding estate taxes over the next two decades, readers who assume that they will have more than $2 million in assets, including their home, needs to consider a QPRT. Greater benefits will be bequeathed to your children as the trust is extended, so this tax strategy will work best for those readers who live in their home for a minimum of 10 years or more.

If you should die before the trust expires, your heirs will be responsible for the estate tax on the current value of the house at the time you die. In determining the value of your home, its current value is not a consideration. Its present value as a future gift is the basis for determining value, enabling you to deeply discount your home and, therefore, its taxes.

A QPRT structure is not without its shortcomings. Your heirs will not avoid capital gains taxes should they sell the property once they inherit it on the initial cost basis. It is possible that parents may outlive their trust and be at the mercy of their children—who, hopefully, will not evict them or raise the rent. If you wish to keep your home in your family, please consult your lawyer, as a QPRT is a complicated tax maneuver.

Reverse mortgages have become increasingly popular as the generation of baby boomers ages, with many wishing to stay in their own homes but desiring to have steady, tax-free income. A reverse mortgage converts the equity in your home into tax-free monthly payments made to you, as a lump sum, or as a line of credit that can be drawn on over a period of years as needed, or a hybrid of such methods. It is available to homeowners at 62 years of age. You gain the benefit of continuing to live in your own home. At the time of your death, your heirs may own the home if they are willing to pay off the reverse mortgage loan, or they can sell the home and use the proceeds to cover the reverse mortgage.

FHA guidelines place limitations on reverse mortgages, depending on the location of your home, its value, your age, and the prevailing interest rate environment. More generous reverse mortgages are available to older seniors, as it is anticipated that they will have shorter life spans. If you are willing to accept higher interest rates, unlimited by FHA reverse mortgage loan guidelines, larger jumbo reverse mortgages are available, although you will not be allowed to exceed the full value of your home.

Readers should be cautioned that reverse mortgages work successfully only if you are prepared to stay in your home for an extended number of years to amortize the costs of the fees, closing costs, insurance, and monthly permit fees. For an FHA reverse mortgage, homeowners will be charged an origination fee of 2 percent of the property value or $2,000, whichever is greater; mandatory mortgage insurance premium adds another 2 percent; and additional fees and closing costs are as much as an additional 3 percent.

Reverse mortgages are not home equity loans, where you must to begin to pay off your loan immediately. Instead, the loan is to be paid only with the proceeds of your home, which will occur either at your death or when you move to a new location. The mortgage company will be paid the sum of all your monthly checks plus interest. If there is a remaining balance, it will be paid to your heirs. If your heirs should prefer retaining your home, they have the option of repaying your reverse mortgage balance.

It is important to know that you will never be in negative territory with a reverse mortgage, as the repayment amount cannot exceed the value of your home at the time you repay it. You will never be placed in a situation where you will be forced to leave your home.

Adriana Dell, a 65-year-old single nurse living in Orlando, Florida, with a $450,000 townhouse, has decided to investigate

Table 6.5   Comparison of FHA and Fannie Mae Reverse Mortgages

	FHA Home Conversion	Fannie Mae Homekeeper
Lump sum at age 65	$122,892	$78,695
Lump sum at age 75	$149,466	$163,464
Monthly advance at 65	$770	$644
Monthly advance at 75	$1,049	$1,419

a reverse mortgage. One of the technicians at her hospital was boasting of his strategy to use the equity in his home as a source of financing to purchase a condominium, hoping to have additional rental income in his retirement.

Adriana was confused by the conversation, as her conservative financial style had always steered her away from accumulating additional debt and she was fearful that using her single largest asset, her home, could well jeopardize a secure retirement. (Review Adriana Dell's profile in Chapter 9.) She considered both an FHA Home Equity Conversion Mortgage and a Fannie Mae HomeKeeper Mortgage. Table 6.5 shows her options.

Berlitz Crash Course: Retiring Abroad

For many approaching retirement, the retirement years are times to do what you have often wished or dreamed of doing. Some people immerse themselves in their hobbies or involve themselves in community activities. Others decide to travel, visiting places that they've previously enjoyed or have always wanted to live. For those retirees excited about traveling internationally or experiencing a different culture and society, living abroad offers many geographic and cost advantages, with a retired couple potentially spending one-third to one-half of what it costs to live in the United States.

When considering offshore locations, Americans value a comfortable climate, moderate housing and living costs, a low crime rate, and political stability. Readers should be cautioned that the quality of healthcare and the availability of medical insurance are equally important, as Medicare is not available abroad. Although nursing care may be cheaper in foreign countries, the quality is suspect, and health insurance coverage may not always be available.

Many Americans living overseas are clueless regarding their tax obligations, believing that if they no longer reside in the country, they no longer need to pay taxes, including taxes on foreign income. However, their tax situation is significantly more complicated. You are required to file a return with the IRS to claim an exclusion of $82,400. If you are considered to still maintain a residence in your home state, you will be required to file state taxes as well. Be prepared to dispose of all property in the United States, if you wish to avoid filing state taxes and plan to visit the United States for no longer than 30 days at a time. Of course, an alternative is to move to a state that does not have an income tax, as explained in the next section.

If you relocate to one of the more than 50 countries that has a tax treaty with the United States, you will receive tax exemptions. Retirees living overseas are also liable for taxes in their new country, although payment of such foreign taxes will serve as a credit for U.S tax purposes. It is important to consult an accounting firm before retiring abroad to properly calculate your tax exposure. IRS publication 593, "Tax Highlights for U.S Citizens and Residents Going Abroad," is another source of information.

Before deciding to retire overseas, it is important to spend sufficient time in the country to understand its cultural and lifestyle issues. Living in the country for a continuous period of three to six months minimum, preferably a year, is highly advisable. Spending a few weeks at a time fails to offer an accurate sense of the dynamics of permanent residence.

Purchasing a home, either an expensive cottage or an estate, requires an understanding of a country's real estate laws. Americans face ownership limits in some countries. Purchase costs can be double that in the United States, with fees running well over 15 percent[15] of the value of the home. In many countries, mortgages are not as available, so the ability to pay in cash is important. Profits from the sale of your home located abroad may be difficult to transfer back to the United States, and such profits will be reduced by foreign capital gains taxes.

It should be noted that readers who choose to live abroad will find it more difficult to actively trade the securities they have in their portfolio and should revisit their portfolio allocation prior to their move. Certainly the tax advantages of municipal bonds should be reconsidered.

Many of the conveniences and amenities taken for granted at home may disappear. Those who cannot live without their Starbucks coffee, Hollywood movies, Borders books, Circuit City, and Seven-11 should not move to the jungles of Central America. Even the most modern cities in another country may be drastically lacking in things you take for granted, but because of the Internet, communication and consumer goods are often just a click away. However, for those who successfully integrate themselves into their second country, the benefits are many.

Tax-Friendly States Beckon

How important is where you live to your financial bottom line? States vary considerably on what taxes they impose and who bears the taxes. Although people living in the United States are uniformly subject to federal taxes, there is a considerable difference in the tax rates among the 50 states. For individuals, the major tax imposed by the federal government is the income tax, and for most people this is the primary focus of tax planning. At the state and local level, however, there is a considerable array of taxes leveled, and the money involved is substantial.

The three largest state taxes for most individuals are the state personal income tax, the state and local sales tax, and the property tax. Inheritance and estate taxes may also be a consideration for those entering their retirement years.

A total of 41 states impose a personal income tax on earnings. Seven states have no personal income tax: Alaska, Florida, Nevada, South Dakota, Texas, Washington, and Wyoming. In addition, two states, New Hampshire and Tennessee, apply the personal income tax only to interest and dividend income. Some states exempt some pension and Social Security income from taxation. Pennsylvania does not tax any retirement income for those over 59½.

Only five states have no sales tax: Alaska, Delaware, Montana, New Hampshire, and Oregon. Sales taxes affect everything from the price of clothes to the price of gasoline—food and medicine are typically excluded from taxation. Sales taxes tend to be the most regressive of taxes. Low-income retirees and workers would generally prefer a progressive income tax and no sales tax.

Although you cannot avoid property taxes, you can find lower rates in some states. The role of the state in property taxes is usually to set the rules of taxation and the maximum rates. Operative rates are, in most cases, determined at the local level. The states with the lowest property tax bills are typically the states with the lowest home values, such as Arkansas and Alabama.

Since property taxes are a primary source of revenue for local governments, low property taxes are often associated with a lack of quality public services. Some states have circuit breakers on property taxes to protect homeowners if home values should soar, although this is typically limited to middle- and lower-income households. In assessing the potential burden of property taxes, it is important to know the maximum rate and how the tax rules would affect you, not only in the year you buy, but in future years.

Recent changes in the federal estate tax law have made inheritance and estate taxes even more complicated at the state level. If estate and inheritance taxes are a primary concern, you should consult your accountant.

Most people first look at the lifestyle benefits of moving and then consider the tax environment. Some may make the mistake of thinking they can create a domicile in a low-tax area while living in their favorite high-tax area. Tax courts frown on this pretense and your favorite high-tax state will see you in court unless the move is real.

For those who are considering a move to reduce their tax burden, the *Bloomberg Wealth Manager* produces an index each year of the states that have the most wealth-friendly tax laws. For 2005, the 10 states that were most friendly to upper income retirees are:

Hawaii, Wyoming, Delaware, Alabama, Louisiana, Nevada, Alaska, Colorado, Washington, and Arizona. The 10 unfriendliest states were Wisconsin, Nebraska, Kansas, Idaho, New York, Maine, Illinois, Minnesota, Missouri, and Texas. Readers can also refer to the Life Calculator's Tax tab for an expanded listing of states by tax level. A comparative cost-of-living index by state is also provided. You are advised to consider both taxes and costs of living when making any relocation decision.

Living Where You Want: Connecting to Where You Need to Be

In a 24/7 wireless world, the workday does not begin or end at the office. For many people, *work* is wherever they choose to conduct business. Whether you spend time at home, overseas, at a vacation resort, or even at Starbucks, connecting to your office and to your files is only a click away if you remain attached to your workplace by e-mail, phone, and Internet.

For those who no longer need to live where they work, the range of housing options is expansive. The decision of where to locate will reflect personal priorities, relationships, interests, hobbies, and life-style comforts, rather than the pressures of an employment situation.

CHAPTER 7

Insurance: Protecting Against Downside Exposure

Financial security and personal wealth are the shared objectives of all readers. Achieving these goals takes more than investment savvy or effective market timing. It requires a comprehensive strategy that is based on a fundamental understanding of your financial position, your risk tolerance, your investment horizon, your willingness to change strategies to meet life's challenges, and the effectiveness of your investment strategy.

A comprehensive strategy cannot be formulated without considering the effect of risk. If you completed the Risk Management exercise in Chapter 1, you should be sensitized to the stark reality that financial security and personal wealth can instantly dissolve due to unexpected adverse events against which you are not insured or have insufficient financial resources to survive. It is vital that you prioritize risk management and engage the necessary level of protection to avoid a loss of your financial security.

You're on Your Own—Employers AWOL on Healthcare Insurance

Healthcare costs and access to quality healthcare are likely to become the civil rights issues of the coming decade, with no positive news in sight. As shown in Figure 7.1, employer health-insurance premiums

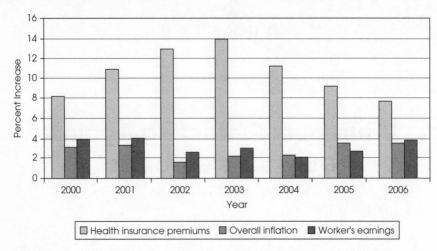

Figure 7.1   Health Premiums Have Increased Faster Than Wages or Inflation

Source: "Employer Health Benefits, 2006 Summary of Findings," Kaiser Family Foundation and Health Research and Educational Trust, www.kff.org/insurance/7527/upload7527.pdf

have risen two times faster than average workers' earnings since 2000.[1] Premiums have increased far more than inflation as a whole. As recently as 2005, 23 percent of adults participating in a national healthcare costs survey stated that they had problems paying medical bills.[2]

Significantly, the concern is shared by both the insured and uninsured. Among the 23 percent expressing anxiety regarding medical bills, 61 percent were insured and 39 percent were not.[3]

Medical debt is linked to personal bankruptcy in more than 50 percent of all cases, averaging $12,000, and occurring even in cases where the debtor had insurance.[4]

Catastrophic healthcare costs can devastate even the most robust of savings plans, rising faster than your ability to pay. Everyone, including public employees, is at risk. In response to rising healthcare costs, employers have passed a greater share of the costs on to their employees, or they have quit providing health coverage altogether.

This exposes workers to more financial risk, confirmed by the following statistics:

- In 2005, 46.6 million Americans (15.9 percent) were without healthcare coverage.[5]
- In 2005, annual premiums for family healthcare totaled $11,480, exceeding the $10,712 gross earnings of a full-time, minimum-wage worker.[6]
- Nearly 9 out of 10 people who considered individual insurance never purchased a plan, as cost of coverage was too high or they were turned down.[7]
- Seniors over 65 are the most pressed by rising health costs, spending almost 13 percent of their income on healthcare, compared to 6 percent by all households.[8]
- Only one in three large employers in 2006 offered retiree medical benefits, down from two in three in 1988.[9]
- Health benefit expenses, the fastest-growing component of employee benefit costs, is a company's third largest expense and is projected to exceed profits within five years.[10]

The fact is indisputable: Uninsured healthcare costs are your greatest financial exposure. Unfortunately, the old system of employer- and government-funded healthcare is obsolete and increasingly bankrupt, leaving you holding the bag. The profile that follows confirms the importance of healthcare insurance in protecting your financial goals.

The Motos wanted to give their son a gift upon his graduation from college. Knowing that he would soon begin his job as an associate at a real estate brokerage firm, they had several options. They could contribute $5,000 toward the purchase of a sporty $20,000 coupe, help finance a $5,000 trip to Europe or Asia, or purchase a health insurance policy, something their son's new job didn't provide, but

(Continued)

which their friend, an actuary, recommended. A two-year policy at $200 a month would cost $4,800. The policy would have a $300 deductible per year, a 20 percent copay, and an out-of-pocket limit of $1,300.* However, their son preferred a car. After all, he said, the car would be much more useful. An insurance policy would be rarely used, if at all, at his young age. The Motos decided to help him purchase the car.

Unfortunately, two years later, their son was involved in a major car accident. He suffered major trauma, including head injuries, shattered vertebrae, and a broken hip. The cost of emergency room treatment, several surgeries, specialist care, and physical and occupational therapy for two years necessary for a full recovery totaled $500,000 over five years. The Motos financed all medical costs out of their retirement savings. If the Motos had purchased health insurance for their son, they would have needed to pay $1,300 out-of-pocket expenses for medical costs related to the accident, $98,700 in co-payments, and $4,800 for two years of insurance premiums. Had their son been insured, the accident would have cost the Motos $104,800, instead of $500,000! The accident caused the Motos to delay their retirement by five years.

*Quote from www.ehealthinsurance.com. HealthPartners PPO plan in the Minneapolis region for a 22-year-old.

Only you can determine how much risk you wish to assume in exchange for lowering your healthcare premium costs. As the scenario for the Motos illustrates, even with health insurance, these costs are not inexpensive. However, they are much more manageable.

Retirees are also being negatively affected by employer-driven trends to reduce benefits. One out of five firms in 2005 required new Medicare-eligible retirees to pay the full cost of their premiums.[11] These employers provide access to the plan, but no financial support. If retirees are required to pay premiums directly, however, they qualify for a tax deduction if their medical expenses, which include premiums, exceed 7.5 percent of their

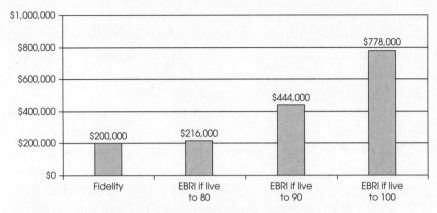

Figure 7.2   Savings Needed for Healthcare by a Retiring 65-Year-Old Couple

Source: Data from *Fidelity Advisor*, October 20, 2006; Paul Fronstin, "Savings Needed to Fund Health Insurance and Healthcare Expenses in Retirement," July 2006 EBRI

adjusted gross income.[12] Figure 7.2 illustrates how much money retirees are likely to need for healthcare expenses, based on how long they live.

Healthcare costs and incidence dramatically increase with age. Average lifetime medical costs after 65 are $225,000 in 2005 dollars, of which Medicare pays $135,000.[13] Seniors over the age of 80 spend 11.5 times more in healthcare costs relative to people between the ages of 50 and 64.[14]

For those with healthcare insurance, higher premiums, larger copayments, and higher annual deductibles will become the norm. Healthcare premiums have consistently grown since 2000 at a rate of more than 7 percent annually. In 2006, employer health insurance premiums increased by 7.7 percent, much faster than that year's inflation rate of 3.5 percent.[15] Healthcare coverage for seniors is even higher, as insurance companies begin to place the retirees into their own high-risk pool, causing premiums to nearly double.

Fortunately, there are strategies that allow you to take control and self-insure against any health problems. Health Reimbursement Accounts allow employers to set aside pretax dollars to cover healthcare expenses. Many employers offer these accounts, combined with high-deductible, lower-premium healthcare insurance, allowing their employees to pay any uncovered expenses with the funds from the health reimbursement account. These funds roll over from year to year and are completely tax-free.

Health savings accounts are a substitute for employer-provided health benefits, which can be funded by a combination of an employer's or employee's tax-free contribution, up to a limit, and must be used in conjunction with a high-deductible, low-premium plan. You can tap funds up to the amount of your insurance deductible or out-of-pocket costs, but cannot exceed $5,250 for an individual or $10,500 for a family. The deductibles were at least $1,050 for individuals and $2,100 for families in 2007.[16] These funds also roll over from year to year and are portable.

The decision to purchase healthcare insurance should focus not only on short-term premium payments but, more important, on long-term health considerations if you have no insurance. The presence of insurance coverage allows access to better, more expensive medical procedures, a large portion of which will be paid through insurance. People not having insurance will opt for a cheaper procedure or choose not to receive medical care. Consequently, they will suffer poor health and higher mortality.[17] People who are uninsured will spend, on average, $1,629 a year on medical expenses. Those who are insured will have medical expenses of $2,975 a year, much of which will be covered by insurance.[18]

Long-term Care Insurance—The Best Investment You'll Make

Long-term care insurance may be the most essential insurance that you purchase. Forecasts indicate that seven out of ten 65-year-olds will require long-term care during their lifetime, with 20 percent requiring two to five years of care and 20 percent requiring more than five years.[19] More than one out of three 65-year-olds[20] will require long-term care in a nursing home or assisted-living facility costing

$75,190 a year for a private room in a nursing home in 2006.[21] It is predicted that those costs will see double-digit increases over the coming years as baby-boomer demand for assisted care creates a shortfall of facilities.

Readers who have liquid assets above $3 million should determine whether they have financial resources to self-insure against the probabilities and potential costs of long-term care. Given the depth of your financial assets, you may be best advised to *not* purchase long-term care insurance, relying on your personal balance sheet to pay the cost of any long-term care needs that may occur. For those readers with assets below $150,000, Medicaid offers a better alternative to long-term care insurance, as they will exhaust their assets and be able to qualify.

Long-term care premiums generally depend on several factors:

- *Term:* the number of years you will receive your benefit payments
- *Benefit amount:* the daily benefit you will receive
- *Elimination period:* the waiting period before you receive your benefits, ranging from 30 days to several months
- *Age at time of purchase:* younger purchasers pay significantly higher premiums after age 60
- *Inflation protection:* the automatic adjustment to keep your benefits, hopefully rising with the cost of care
- *Flexibility:* using long-term care insurance to support home care workers in your home

There will be trade-offs between the cost of insurance and the level of coverage. A three-year policy with a $200 daily benefit, a 90-day waiting period, purchased at age 55 will cost $1,080 annually, compared to a similar policy bought at age 65 for $2,168, an increase of 100 percent.[22]

Likewise, a lifetime policy with a 30-day waiting period bought at age 55 with a $200 a day daily benefit and a 5 percent compounded inflation factor will cost $4,624 annually, but $8,000 at age 65, an increase of 73 percent. The older you are at the time you purchase the policy, the more expensive the policy premium. Most consumers select policies with three to five years of coverage and a 60-to-90 day waiting period, assuming that they will not need longer-term care over an extended period and can afford to pay for initial periods of care out of their savings.

Before you choose your provider, check the company's S&P and Amvest ratings to evaluate future financial stability. You should recognize that you will be paying for long-term care insurance for 15 to 25 years before you actually use the policy. Although companies still must honor contracts, even if they are no longer in the business, the quality of customer service will certainly suffer. You are strongly advised to check the fine print on the contract. Are all forms of care-giving, whether home care, assisted care, hospice, or respite care covered? What medical conditions would prevent your eligibility for long-term care insurance? How frequent are premium increases?

If you have an increased risk of chronic conditions, such as cancer, diabetes, or heart conditions, or if you have a disability or Alzheimer's that may leave you requiring care services, you should purchase long-term care insurance. Usually the premiums are higher after the age of 60, and you may not pass the medical eligibility requirements for this insurance.

You must consider the financial trade-offs of purchasing a lower-priced policy in your 40s or early 50s, when you are less likely to be denied coverage for health reasons, but will assume premium costs for many years when you are unlikely to require long-term care insurance. Ideally, you should consider purchasing long-term care insurance while in your mid- to late 50s, once other large-expense items, such as college expenses, have been taken care of.

One strategy is to purchase the most basic coverage and add additional benefits later, if you can't afford comprehensive coverage now. However, policies that allow you to amend benefits later, such as inflation protection, will price these options at the age when they are added, increasing the expense beyond the cost if initially included. All readers should seriously weigh incorporating a cost-of-living inflator and a cap on annual premium increases as potential elements of whatever policy they purchase.

Additionally, some of the newer long-term care insurance policies may give you a spousal discount on a separate policy or may allow you to share benefits with your spouse on a single policy. If you have life insurance, your policy provider may even allow you to exchange your cash-value life-insurance policy for a combination life-insurance/long-term care insurance policy that deducts any long-term care payments from the death benefit received by your heirs. This exchange is tax free and usually more cost effective than buying a new combination policy.

As of 2007, taypayers ages 71 and older can claim $3,680 per person in tax deductions. Those ages 61 to 70 can claim $2,950; ages 50 to 60 can claim $1,110; ages 40 to 50 can claim $550; and individuals less 40 can claim $290 for tax-free payouts of $260 a day.[23]

Readers should carefully review the selected Web sites that are referenced at the end of this book to answer those questions, prior to speaking with insurance brokers regarding policies. The more informed you are regarding the significance of each of the above questions and, importantly, your own personal requirements and preferences, the better shopper you will be for long-term care insurance. Do not be persuaded by a broker to purchase a policy that does not include the protections that are vital to your sense of comfort.

For those over 65 with assets, Medicare provides access to health services, discounted prescriptions, and medical care for short-term illnesses. However, it will not cover custodial care costs, such as nursing homes or assisted living. To cover this exposure, readers with assets between $150,000 and $2 million should seriously consider long-term care insurance as part of their financial planning. If it is their intention to leave an estate to their family, it is vital to their financial security that they have long-term care insurance to cover an extended period in assisted care so they do not deplete their estate.

As many as half of those 65 and over will face no out-of-pocket expenses for long-term care, choosing to rely on Medicaid.[24] To become for eligible for Medicaid, your resources must fall below $2,000, not including your home and car. The states of New York,

California, Connecticut, and Indiana will, however, allow you to protect up to $100,000 in assets while allowing you to access Medicaid through their Partnership for Long-Term Care programs. One family's experience with long-term care insurance is profiled below.

When Emma Sprint was widowed at 57, she sold her home and moved in with her daughter and son-in-law, Trudy and Hank Trio, to assist them in raising their five children, enabling her daughter to work part-time. She placed the proceeds from the sale of her modest home into a trust fund for her grandchildren's college education, but wisely chose to purchase high-quality healthcare and long-term care insurance for herself, preferring to not be a burden on her family. Buying coverage at age 57 in good health, Emma was able to receive a lower premium than if she had waited until future years.

Emma urged Hank's parents to also consider purchasing long-term care insurance as a couple. They did not wish to pay the annual premiums beginning at age 60, preferring to place their money into a new business enterprise and expecting that it would provide sufficient profits to make them financially secure.

Unfortunately, by their late 60s, both of Hank's parents had become infirm. Hank's mother was diagnosed with diabetes and his father was showing early signs of Alzheimer's. By their 70s, his parents had moved to an assisted facility, but found it necessary to move to a higher level of care, necessitating greater expense. Recognizing that their rapidly declining financial resources would be depleted within the immediate future, Hank and Trudy decided to have the couple move in with them and hired home care aides to care for all three elderly parents.

The elder Trios were very fortunate that they had family that would supplement the cost of their care. However, they did impose a financial cost on their family, resulting in a delayed retirement of five years to finance the additional cost of home care for the elder Trios. Had the senior Trios purchased long-term care insurance, they would have been able to continue to support themselves independently, protected from the worst of these costs.

Disability Insurance—More Important than You Realize

Disability insurance, only available to those who are working, is insurance that will replace a portion of your income in the event that you become unable to work. Receiving it from your employer and/or supplementing it with a privately provided policy, you may elect to purchase either short-term or long-term disability insurance.

Although you certainly are strongly advised to purchase both healthcare and long-term care insurance to reduce your medical costs, it is also important to consider your exposure to disability risk. Given that you have a one in eight chance of becoming disabled during the course of your employment[25] and a 52 percent chance after age 65,[26] you should consciously measure whether you wish to hedge the risk of disability through the purchase of disability insurance.

Is it cost effective for you to pay a premium for disability insurance, or are you financially better protected by transferring a similar amount of dollars into an investment account that will generate replacement income if you are disabled? The principal and earned interest of such investment funds may well serve as your own self-insured account to cover short-term disability exposure. Most working individuals will be able to access unused vacation and sick time to also ensure a flow of income during a limited period of disability.

Long-term disability insurance, which can begin paying as early as the 31st day following your injury, is, for most readers, a more cost-effective option. The loss of income over an uncertain period extending perhaps several years is an effective argument for long-term disability insurance coverage.

In evaluating the decision to purchase long-term disability insurance, readers should weigh their ability to withstand a loss of employment income beyond their vacation and sick-day benefits. While the chances of long-term disability are considerably lower than short-term incidents, the economic damage of being without any income for several months, or even years, may not be a risk that you wish to assume.

Recent (2004) statistics confirm a grim reality: 12 percent of the workforce ages 21 to 64 have a disability.*,[27] Disability insurance providers report that the majority of disabilities are not caused by accidents. In fact, only 10 percent of long-term disability claims and 13 percent of short-term claims result from injuries.[28]

One major disability supplement that cannot be ignored is Social Security Disability Insurance. However, in order to receive SSDI, you must have a long-lasting—at least one year—disability, or a disability that will result in death that prevents you from making more than a certain dollar amount per month. In 2006, this was $860.

Another type of disability benefit comes in the form of worker's compensation, which all states require employers to provide. However, this type of coverage is limited to injuries or illnesses related to the job, meaning that most disability-related events are not covered.**,[29] Workers receive benefits usually equal to two-thirds of income, but this may be lower, depending on state maximums.

Anti-aging Science and Virtual Medicine

Successful protection against adverse events you will encounter does not imply that you should limit yourself to financial instruments. You can greatly increase your chances of longevity and health by taking care of yourself mentally and physically. As we move into the future, a plethora of new technologies will make this job even easier than you can imagine.

Virtual medical checkups will increasingly become the norm. You can save time and money by monitoring your bio-signs through telemedicine providers sending this information wirelessly to your doctor. You are able to monitor your blood pressure, heart rate, and even weight. This technology can be used for conditions such as diabetes,

---

*Disability: Refer to definition on page 62.

** 2002 U.S. Group Disability Rate and Risk Management Survey, 2003, National Safety Council and JHA, Less than 4 percent of long-term disabilities were caused by on-the-job injuries.

heart failure, depression, and post-traumatic stress, instantly sending updates about your health every few minutes to a medical provider. Virtual medicine is so effective that the Veterans Administration has planned to double the number of people on telemedical home care to over 20,000 by 2007.[30]

In today's world, you can even take a picture with a webcam and send it over the Internet to a doctor, or call a 24-hour phone doctor and hear back within three hours. Online you will also be able to request prescription refills, review X-rays and lab tests, schedule appointments, have an online consultation, update your medical conditions, and share your patient records through the Electronic Medical Record System, provided by many service providers. The Electronic Medical System integrates all your information and provides real-time access to care providers, hospitals, labs, and pharmacies.

What will really enable you to age well? Experts all commonly agree that the major determinants of how you will do later on in your life include: a good diet, controlling your weight, watching your cholesterol, exercise, good genes, social relationships with friends and family, and getting enough sleep, which helps to lower your overall stress.

What are the traits of successful agers? They hare flexibility, optimism, interest in new things, and a good sense of humor. Successful seniors are not loners. They have an extended family and a network of friends. For men, being married will help, but for women, marital status is irrelevant.

Life Insurance You May Outlive—or Sell for Cash

A major part of your fiscal checkup should be an evaluation of life insurance. For baby boomers and Generation-Xers, life insurance may denote a product that would be best left to those engaging in lawn bowling and senior citizen bridge clubs. Today's life insurance policies are, however, effective retirement planning tools that can bridge the gap between increased longevity and decreased savings.

Using the Life Calculator, readers can perform a risk/return analysis, evaluating whether life insurance and/or annuity products add value to their portfolio.

Life insurance, purchased either individually or as a member of a company policy, provides income replacement for your dependents in the event that you pass away. Without your income and with limited savings, your spouse and children may be exposed to a serious reduction in lifestyle or, worse, bankruptcy. Given that Social Security survivorship benefits are not available until age 60, life insurance becomes the bridge between your death and your spouse's eligibility for such benefits.

Funeral, burial, probate, and real estate costs can also be financed through insurance benefits. Additionally, some insurance policies can provide emergency liquidity, as they have a cash value that can be borrowed against or withdrawn, if not paid out as a benefit.

Life insurance now masquerades as a variety of new products offering death benefits, emergency cash, inflation protection, and a guaranteed stream of income. Such insurance products can be structured as a traditional term policy, a return of premium policy, or a customized product, reflecting your income and medical needs. The two main categories of life insurance are permanent life insurance, which insures you for life, or term life insurance, which will insure you for a set amount of time.

Permanent Life Insurance

A permanent life insurance policy provides lifelong protection. The premium in this type of policy remains the same, but is higher than term life insurance, as there is a savings account coupled with it. There are three permanent life insurance options: whole, adjustable, and variable policies.

1. *Whole life.* The most common life insurance policy pays a death benefit and increases the cash value of your policy at a set rate.
2. *Adjustable life.* You have several options, such as increasing your death benefit or altering your premium payments by using money from your cash value balance.

3. *Variable life.* This policy allows you to select the investment mix of your cash value balance. Although your cash value balance and death benefit may decrease if you suffer investment losses, some companies will still guarantee a minimum death benefit.

Term Life Insurance

A second major form of life insurance is a term policy. It pays if death occurs during the term of the policy. Terms can range from 1 to 30 years, or up to a specified age. Level term policies have a constant death benefit. Decreasing term policies have a benefit drop each year, or over some designated time period, which can help pay for decreasing financial obligations. Level term benefits are intended for those who want to provide income for a surviving spouse and children. Such insurance is generally bought by younger parents. Decreasing term benefit insurance is for those who are concerned not so much with a savings shortfall, but rather, with specific payment obligations, such as a mortgage.

Who qualifies for life insurance? One does not have to be in perfect health to qualify for a life insurance policy. There are policies available for people with medical problems, such as breast or prostate cancer, heart disease, and diabetes. Premium payments are based on a person's age and physical condition at the initiation of the policy, usually staying the same throughout the term of the policy. Most policies will not provide insurance past 80 years of age.

A new form of term life insurance policy, return of premium (ROP) insurance, will pay you if you outlive the term of your life insurance. Intended for younger, healthy individuals who are certain to continue paying their premiums, this insurance policy is highly attractive, generating an average return of roughly 6 percent if held to the end of the term.[31] At the end of the term, insurance companies will return either all or a portion of the premium, without interest.

Most companies that offer this feature require that the policy be in effect for the entire term. If you die before the end of the term, your beneficiaries receive the normal life insurance payout, but not the premium return. Those who are fortunate to outlive their life insurance receive the bonus premium payment. Surprisingly, all of the ROP refund is nontaxable, including the premium return.

Life insurance is an investment vehicle that always has a market value. Rather than letting a policy lapse, if you find that you can no longer pay the premium or have determined that the coverage is not worth the cost, you can choose to sell your outstanding policy for a percentage of its value, depending on the number of years remaining in its term and your life expectancy.

Structuring a sale of your policy under those circumstances, you would enter a life settlement agreement with an investor who buys the policy and takes over the payments. When you die, the investor receives the benefit. You can use your lump-sum payment to further your financial security buying long-term care insurance, adding to your investments, or paying an outstanding bill. Investors will only purchase your life insurance policies if your policy is over $250,000 and if it appears that you will not live much longer. On average, you may expect to receive 20 percent of the policy's face value, as the investor bears the longevity risk.

If you are experiencing a terminal illness and are short of financial resources needed for the quality medical care you desire, it is possible to structure the sale of your insurance policy to obtain immediate cash resources. Defined as a viatical settlement, this sale reaps a higher percentage return, generally 50 to 80 percent of the face value of your insurance policy[32] with the value determined on the length of your remaining life. The decision to cash out your policy assures that your medical expenses do not leave extraordinary debt for your family and heirs to finance. Patients utilizing this approach have determined that it is far better to pay for their medical costs than to leave a life insurance settlement to their heirs.

Longevity Insurance

For those who do not have the option of a defined benefit plan, an annuity may replace the uncertainty of any future income with guaranteed payments beginning immediately or at some date in the future. You purchase an annuity contract from an insurance company, paying a lump sum or a series of payments now for a stream of income payments like a defined benefit plan. An annuity has the benefit of insuring you against longevity risk, the risk that you will deplete your retirement assets by living longer than expected.

An immediate annuity will have income payments begin immediately, while a deferred annuity will have the payments begin sometime in the future. There are two types of annuities classified under those categories, fixed and variable. A fixed annuity guarantees a minimum growth rate of your annuity balance between the time of your purchase and when your first future payment begins. The future payments are guaranteed to be a certain amount depending on your balance at that time. Depending on the length of time over which you choose to receive your payments, your annuity may cost less now. The most expensive option possible is a perpetual annuity, where you will receive payments until you die.

For more flexibility, you may wish to consider a variable annuity. This type of policy allows you to invest your purchase payments among different options for a chance of greater upside income potential. However, with this upside comes greater uncertainty, as your returns and payments can vary depending on how the investments picked perform.

If you choose to purchase what is known as an equity-indexed annuity, you will receive a return linked to the performance of an index and will be guaranteed at least a minimum return. This way, if your investments do poorly, you will still be assured of income during retirement.

One of the largest benefits of annuity contracts is the tax-deferred treatment of any investment gains. The gains are taxed only when you begin to take money out of the annuity. However, the payments will be taxed at the income tax bracket rather than at capital gains rates. Depending on your income, this may or may not be a better choice for you. Since variable annuities are securities, they are regulated by the Securities and Exchange Commission (SEC). Index annuities may or may not be regulated.

Another feature of an annuity that you can pay for is the death benefit. This option allows you to designate a beneficiary who will receive either your current account balance with investment gains or the sum of current payments made in the purchase of the annuity.

Annuity providers generally do not like it if you withdraw income from a deferred annuity immediately after purchase, as they lose money if this occurs. In order to prevent this, many annuities have withdrawal charges or surrender fees that gradually decrease as you get closer to the payment period of the annuity. However, some insurers allow you to annually withdraw a certain portion of the funds in your annuity without charges, but this may increase the cost of the annuity.

Other features are guaranteed minimum payments, even if you do not have the account balance to support the payments. Recently, annuity providers have also begun pairing annuities with other types of insurance, including long-term care.

Estate Planning: Taking Care of Those You Care About

Being born wealthy is no assurance of a secure financial future. Six out of 10 affluent families will lose the family fortune by the end of the second generation and 9 out of 10 by the third generation.[33] Between 1998 and 2052, $41 trillion will be bequeathed by all generations.[34] Estate planning clearly will be valuable for you and your family, if you wish to pay as few taxes as possible and insure that your bequest is trouble free.

Although there is a great deal of uncertainty regarding estate planning due to constant changes in federal and state taxes, some things are certain. The estate tax is one of the highest taxes that will be levied on you, reaching nearly 50 percent depending on your circumstances. Congress has recently taken some steps to amend this situation. By 2008, you will be protected from federal and state taxes if your estate is under $2 million. In 2009, the limit will increase to $3.5 million. The tax disappears in 2010 and will be reinstated in 2011 for estates more than $1 million.

For an unquestioned transfer of assets, you will need a will prepared by an estate planning lawyer who is a member of the bar or estate and trust committee. You should know their fees (flat or hourly) and know their experience with estates of your size. However, be careful when assigning power of attorney to others, whether in your family, to your lawyer, or to your broker, as they can commit fraud. It is particularly important to not transfer such powers of attorney to paid caregivers. Note that a healthcare power of attorney is separate but equally important, in the event that you become unable to communicate your health needs.

In family discussions, your family members should review the actions upon your death. This should include:

- Funeral arrangements
- Locations of safes, keys, wills, and important documents
- Name and contact information for designated executors
- Investment account information including bank accounts, safe deposit accounts, life insurance policies, and broker contacts
- Title documents for any real estate owned
- Update beneficiary designation to reflect changing marital status and changing ages of beneficiaries

Despite the hype that baby boomers will inherit huge amounts of money, recent studies have repeatedly reported that the typical sum received is less than $70,000, with a slim 7.5 percent receiving more than $100,000.[35] If you are among the lucky few to inherit money, this inheritance may become the salvation you need for your retirement security. The largest amount of inheritance will be received by an extremely finite number of already wealthy families. When receiving an inheritance, beware of taking any action for a year, consult an advisor to review the tax impact of a bequest before making any expenditure, and evaluate all investment opportunities before jumping at an immediate scheme.

8

Meet the Forties and the Fifties: Fearless and Fantastic Years

The Life Calculator is a powerful tool to support lifelong financial planning. Its ability to anticipate and measure the effects of life's many changes gives you the ability to address the variables of real life and project a realistic picture of your future.

Although I urge you to use the Life Calculator to create an initial personal profile, I think it is equally educational to read the life profiles of hypothetical families and individuals whose life experiences may mirror your own. Reading their responses to financial challenges can provide meaningful direction in your own life. All the financial analysis in the profiles is provided courtesy of the Life Calculator.

These profiles depict individuals or couples at a specific point in their life journeys. They incorporate the adverse events and opportunities that have or will occur, the financial impacts of these events, and the actions taken by the hypothetical individual or couple to mitigate their results or maximize their good fortune.

Forties Decade: Child Rearing and Career Advancement

This decade is marked by a focus on career advancement and on child rearing for those of you who have families. Concentration on careers reflects the statistical reality that the 40s are defining periods

131

during which earnings are significantly increased and, in the case of those in the corporate arena, promotions may well define the extent to which one's career is expected to advance.

This is the ideal life-cycle period to measure your satisfaction with your current job environment and to reevaluate other careers, industries, or potential employers. The Life Calculator's "Career" resource tab can provide direction on potential jobs, salaries, and benefits. If a change in job or industry is desired to improve your financial security, health, and retirement benefits or job stability, you are strongly advised to take actions to pursue those changes within this decade. Opportunities are far more plentiful during this decade, when potential employers will still view you as having highly productive years ahead. You are also less likely to face negative age bias.

If a parent, the reader should establish college funds, evaluate public versus private educational opportunities, and purchase comprehensive health insurance for your family. Parents with few financial resources are advised to consider life insurance to protect against the likelihood of disability and/or early death.

You will be aggressive during this decade in allocating financial resources to maximize earnings. Given the high-expense/low-savings ratio for most readers during this lifestyle period, you will be particularly vulnerable to bumps in inflation and earnings losses. Please review the Investments tab on the Life Calculator to better understand the historical patterns of both inflation and market returns.

Forties Profiles

The Newtons: Former Entrepreneurs—Uncertain Cash Flows Result in Changed Careers

- Marla and Bill Newton: Atlanta, Georgia
- Ages 46 and 48
- Marla earns $55,000, Bill earns $115,000
- Twins, 10 years old

- Challenges:
  - ◆ Volatile income
  - ◆ Lack of pensions
- Child care expenses
- College expenses
- Caring for aging parents
- Uninsured healthcare costs for child

Marla and Bill Newton, married for 14 years, are the parents of 10-year-old twins. Marla, prior to having her children, worked in human resources for a Fortune 500 company, while Bill worked in marketing and sales for a pharmaceutical company.

Marla's choice to be a stay-at-home mother until her children entered kindergarten coincided with her husband's decision to join his brother, a real estate executive, in forming a real estate investment trust (REIT). Bill became a real estate broker and assumed responsibilities for sales and marketing functions of the company, building a staff of sales agents to secure tenants for their luxury properties located throughout the southeastern United States.

Although Bill appreciated his opportunity to earn high compensation in the early years, the real estate market began to experience saturation of properties during the past two years, and he did not foresee an opportunity to maintain the level of income he enjoyed in his earlier well-compensated years. His uncertain revenues left him unable to plan for future financial obligations.

Job flexibility was the highest priority for Marla as she returned to work when the twins were five. Her goal was to both fund her sons' college educations and to provide the money for a family investment account.

Rather than returning to the corporate sector, she chose the entrepreneurial route, establishing a nanny employment agency with a former business colleague. The hours, though flexible, proved to be demanding, with frequent late nights and weekends, required to interview candidates and meet parents.

Frustrated by their lack of personal time, often conflicted by family obligations and uncertain of their future income, the Newtons began discussing whether they should both remain in the volatile entrepreneurial sector. They decided to test what-if alternative work scenarios using this book's Life Calculator.

The Newtons wanted to project what their financial position would be 4, 8, and 20 years from now. Looking forward in four years to the possibility of transferring their sons to private school in ninth grade, financing their children's college educations in eight years, caring for aging parents, and affording their own retirements—as early as 20 years from now—Marla and Bill realized the value of a stable income. They decided to consider selling their business interests and returning to corporate positions, with the hope of having more secure incomes, better retirement benefits, and more regular work hours.

Bill's compensation over the past 10 years has ranged from $100,000 to $170,000 annually, averaging $130,000. Marla's income, after business expenses, ranged from $45,000 to $65,000, averaging $55,000. For the five years during which both spouses have been working, their highest income occurred in 2003, when they reported $200,000—the same year they bought their home for $700,000 using a $175,000 down payment, drawn from the appreciation on their first home and from taking early withdrawals on their 401(k) funds. The couple spent $100,000 in upgrades, in furnishing their new home, and in landscaping the property.

Always assuming that future years would bring increased income opportunities, the couple has never created a family budget or set investment goals. Their current $60,000 diversified portfolio has experienced principal losses while averaging a return of 5 percent. Given their current spending of $30,000 for full-time live-in child care to accommodate their extended work schedules; a $6,900 annual car payment; annual mortgage payments of $40,000 on their $525,000 30-year mortgage (6.5 percent); property and income taxes; and generous living expenses, the Newtons will have to draw down $19,700 from their savings for the four years that they require child care until their children are of high school age. Neither spouse has a pension. Their savings have not been matched by employer contributions.

Marla realizes, in considering job options, that she can save $30,000 a year in child care expenses if she takes a nine-to-five job, freeing her weekends and evenings. She will also save the almost $10,000 annual loss in savings that, over four years, would add have added $40,000 to their accounts. In job interviews with a school district, she recognizes the value of employer-matched contributions, a more comprehensive healthcare plan than they currently have through her husband's employment, and paid vacations—all attractive benefits she does not receive in her self-employed position.

She accepts the job in a regional high school, working as a guidance counselor, teaching freshman health, and coaching the girls' softball team for extra compensation—a sport she herself played in college. She earns the same as before, $55,000 a year, while working the same hours her children are in school. If she had continued to work as an entrepreneur with irregular hours until her sons entered high school, she would have needed $120,000 in that four-year period to pay her $30,000 annual nanny expenses.

Bill is pleased with Marla's new employment and is determined to consider his own alternatives. His long hours at the REIT in an increasingly competitive real estate market have not resulted in the additional income he had expected, and they have reduced his time with the family.

Bill interviews with a large corporation seeking a real estate manager and secures the position, paying $115,000 a year. Although it pays significantly less than he made in his best years in the REIT, the position nets him more after-tax money with its generous benefit package, including a high-quality healthcare plan and employer-matched savings. It allows him to reduce his workweek from 60 hours to 45 hours. Most important, it guarantees a set income from which he can budget.

Although Marla and Bill are earning less after-tax income of $136,140 (compared to $150,540), they gain a positive cash flow by not having to pay for a nanny, having a pension for Marla, and having employer-matched savings of $10,000—not to mention less stress.

If the Newtons save just $6,000 a year, with an employer-matched savings plan doubling that figure, at the end of a four-year period their retirement account would have grown from its current $60,000 to $123,860. If they had remained entrepreneurs, they would have drawn down on their savings and their nest egg would be $29,068—a difference in four years of $94,792—a great incentive to take the new positions. This money can either be used for retirement or for their children's college educations.

If the money remains in their retirement accounts, in 19 years, when Bill retires at age 68, the Newtons will have amassed $783,677 in retirement savings—$139,075 more than they would have if they were entrepreneurs. That $139,075 represents the full funding of nearly two additional retirement years at a spending level of $83,540. Along with their Social Security and Marla's pension, 80 percent of her final salary, they can expect to live comfortably for the remainder of their lives with sufficient surplus at the end, leaving a potential estate for their children, even with an inflation rate of 3 percent. This is in stark contrast to their financial position, if they had remained entrepreneurs, with their wealth depleted by Bill's 78th birthday.

The Newtons face a difficult emotional and financial decision. How do they strike a balance between paying the cost of their children's college educations and saving money for their own retirement? Are they able to afford both? Further complicating this financial decision is the Newtons' consideration of the need to support Bill's aging mother, who may have inadequate savings to finance her expensive medical and nursing home costs due to her Alzheimer's condition.

Many baby boomers face the same stark reality as the Newtons. They have become the sandwich generation: caring for their aging parents, saving for their own retirements, and funding their children's college educations, all within overlapping years. In prior generations, families had the near certainty of an employer-funded retirement and had their children when they were in their 20s and early 30s. Their children's college payments were completed earlier in their careers, leaving them more time to fund their retirements.

Using the Life Calculator, the Newtons recognize the importance of continuing to save for their retirement. They decide to cap the amount of dollars they are willing to contribute to each of their son's college education. Their sons would most likely attend public universities and would need to supplement the Newtons' 529 college fund with loans and part-time jobs. The Newtons' goal is to save $100,000 for each son's education.

The Newtons are sophisticated in their awareness that their first obligation is to create a well-funded retirement account. Neither care of an aging parent nor saving for their children's college educations should jeopardize their own retirement security. In fact, the greatest gift the Newtons can give their children is the assurance that they will never need to rely on them for financial support.

The Newtons are cautious. They decide to test the effects of caring for Bill's aging widowed mother who has not been so fortunate in her retirement savings and who will require funding for healthcare or nursing home expenses when she is older. The Newtons' use the Life Calculator to measure the financial effect that taking care of an aging parent would have on their retirement. They conservatively assume that they would need to allocate $30,000 annually for 10 years, with the expenses beginning when Bill is 60.

After running the numbers, they note that their retirement account will be depleted by Bill's age 77 and Marla's age 75. They decide that this is an acceptable risk to their finances, as Bill's mother may not require such extended financial support. If the Newtons should need to provide financial support to Bill's mother, substantially denting their over half a million dollars of savings, they still will have the substantial equity from their home. If necessary, the Newtons will consider a reverse mortgage to provide additional income support to Marla's age 90.

Six years later, at Bill's age 54 and before assuming any responsibility for parental care, one of their twin sons is involved in a ski accident. The Newtons' unreimbursed total out-of-pocket healthcare costs total $40,000 over one year. Rerunning the Life Calculator, the Newtons discover that they will deplete their savings account by Bill's age 72 and Marla's age 70.

After reviewing his financial options by using the Life Calculator, Bill decides to extend his employment until age 70 and projects that they will have $319,825 in their retirement account. This decision will extend the Newtons' savings to his age 81 and Marla's age 79. If they reduce their retirement spending by 10 percent, the Newtons could potentially extend their savings to ages 87 and 85 respectively. Moreover, if Bill's mother does not require all the funds the Newtons have earmarked for her care, their retirement wealth should last them for their lifetime.

The decision by the Newtons to change their entrepreneurial careers to more stable employment allowed them to build their savings to a level capable of financing the adverse events they may encounter, as well as preparing for their retirement. Congratulations, Newtons on mastering Rule #2: Focus on Reducing Risk! The Newtons' financial picture is shown in Tables 8.1 and 8.2.

Table 8.1   Potential Retirement Accounts—No Adverse Events

By Year:	Entrepreneurial	Corporate	Difference
2010	$27,000	$160,000	$133,000
2014	$143,950	$303,680	$159,720
2027	$664,180	$965,180	$301,000

Table 8.2   Newtons' Timeline

Date	2007–2011	2012	2013	2014–2018	2019–2027	2028
Notable Events	Switch to corporate jobs; $30,000 annual savings for nanny	End car payments	Son in ski accident		Reserve money to care for parent with Alzheimer's; Marla retires (2026)	Bill retires

Blackboard: Recently Promoted Executive Director
of a Nonprofit Healthcare Organization, Attempting
to Adopt a Child and Purchase a Home

- Vivian Blackboard: Denver, Colorado
- Age 40, divorced
- Income of $89,000
- Challenges:
  - Disability
  - Past poor credit due to excessive consumer debt remaining from marriage
  - Lack of pension
  - Purchase of a home

Vivian Blackboard has had a challenging past five years, having being diagnosed with a chronic disease; experiencing a job change; divorcing; and relocating to a new city. Her medical condition, lupus, ended her accountancy career in Los Angeles. The frequent leaves of absence and hospitalizations had taken their toll on her and her client relationships. Under the advice of her doctor, she sought a less stressful job. Vivian's marriage also dissolved four years ago, as a result of the stress of her illness. Upon her divorce, she chose to move back to Denver, where she had been raised and where her extended family still lived.

Given her health condition, Vivian sought an employment opportunity that both provided healthcare insurance and work flexibility to enable her to have the necessary time off when her condition was provoked. Fortunately, Vivian found work at a nonprofit healthcare organization where she was valued as its Chief Financial Officer. She was recently promoted to the position of Executive Director with a generous salary increase to $89,000. As a nonprofit, the pay scale was not as tempting as a corporate position, but Vivian was attracted to its healthcare benefits and time flexibility.

Over the past few years, Vivian has lived a meager lifestyle, with the focus on paying off the last of her consumer debt remaining from her previous marriage and the outstanding balance of her MBA loans. Her objective has been to improve her credit

Table 8.3   Vivian Blackboard's Timeline

	2002	2003–2006	2007	2032
Notable Events	Diagnosed with Lupus	Divorce Moved back to Denver New career with MBA	Purchase of new home Adoption	Vivian retires

history to qualify to purchase a home and to adopt a child: her two life goals.

Vivian has long wished to become a mother and has, for the past three years, been exploring options to adopt a child. She was recently extremely excited to learn that her adoption application has been approved, following an extended review of her health (her lupus condition is well controlled), employment, and credit references. As a Hispanic who wishes to adopt a multiracial child, she has been assured that she will have a baby before the end of next year.

Her other life goals are to purchase a $350,000 two-bedroom townhouse in a redevelopment area, where she will receive the benefit of a subsidized mortgage. She plans to save a maximum of $6,000 in her employer's 401(k) plan to provide financial security for her and her new child, expecting to need $400,000 in savings to support her child through college. As a single mother, Vivian realizes the serious financial responsibility she is assuming as the sole provider of her child. Her recently retired mother and father have enthusiastically agreed to provide child care for her baby, so that Vivian can continue to work full-time following the adoption. Congratulations, Vivian, on Rule #1: Owning Your Future and on your new family and home!

The Razors: Law Enforcement and Public Attorney—Limited Income, but Strong Retirement Security

- James and Nancy Razor: Greensboro, North Carolina
- Ages 43 and 40
- Nancy earns $75,000 and James earns $62,000
- Two children, 6 and 2

- Challenges:
  - Cash flow pressure
  - Care of an aging parent
  - College expenses

James and Nancy Razor met at a city function in Greensboro, North Carolina, where Nancy worked as an analyst and James as a police officer. Now both are in mid-level positions, Nancy as an Assistant City Attorney and James as an Investigations Commander.

As public employees, they have a defined benefit plan that will provide 80 percent of their last combined salaries of $109,600, or $87,680, from their retirements at age 65, 22 years in the future for James and 25 years for Nancy. They are comfortable knowing that they will be able to fund an active retirement of travel, a second vacation home, and their dream of purchasing, renovating, and operating a bed and breakfast hotel in the Blue Ridge Mountains. Their after-tax incomes of $51,000 and $60,753 is sufficient to meet their conservative spending of $101,500.

Whenever James's younger brother, Ted, visits, the conversation invariably turns to Ted's employer, Delta Airlines. Ted is an extravagant bachelor who has a reputation of squiring women in every exotic city he visits. Although he earns more than $200,000 annually as a pilot, he hasn't established any savings or investment goals, relying on his corporate pension for future retirement. Now that his airline is in bankruptcy and is threatening to freeze the pension program, he is worried that his promised retirement package might disappear. Ted is devastated at the likely loss of his pension.

Ted's uncertain financial future is particularly unsettling to James and Nancy, as they had hoped he would contribute to the costs of caring for his mother, Theresa, who has recently been diagnosed with Alzheimer's disease and will need the increasing support of a live-in caregiver in her home or a form of assisted living as her disease progresses. She has no long-term care insurance, must rely on restricted payments from Medicare, and is now unable to secure any supplemental insurance. She has limited income from an annuity and sold her larger home years earlier to help pay her husband's uninsured healthcare costs of private-duty nurses during his hospitalization for a stroke. Her current townhouse is her remaining asset, and she had been working part-time to supplement her Social Security income.

The Razors have learned from Theresa's doctor that it is likely that she may live another 10 years, with accelerated deterioration within the next 3 years. The family has vowed to let Theresa live at home as long as medically possible. It now appears that James and Nancy will have to shoulder Theresa's care themselves.

Although the Razors do not face the anxiety and financial shortfalls that many boomers will realize at retirement, they have three demanding cash-flow challenges:

1. They must budget for the care of James's mother. They will initially contribute $15,000 a year to support a $30,000 caregiver in her home for the first three years. Having reviewed the adverse events costs summary detailed in Chapter 4, they project a cost of $50,000 for nursing home care. A portion will be paid by other sources for the expected remaining 10 or more years, however, so they will only need to pay $30,000.
2. They wish to send both of their children to private colleges beginning in 2018—one after the other for eight years—with an expected average annual cost of $60,000, projecting a 3 percent inflationary factor on today's private college cost of $35,000.
3. If they do not wish to cut back on their current lifestyle during retirement, they must also accumulate enough savings to finance the 20 percent difference between their 80 percent pensions and their current income.

Using the Life Calculator, the Razors will be able to view the financial consequences of their decisions. Their most critical period is the next 20 years. During that time, they will need to finance expensive caregiver costs for Theresa and fund their children's college education. The Razors decide to retire at age 55 from their current jobs and take second jobs, doing similar work at the same salary level, while collecting their pensions. Their retirement goal of having 100 percent of preretirement income is easily met through the significant earnings from their second jobs—much of which can be saved as they are able to receive pension income.

James and Nancy face many anxious and difficult moments in the demanding years 2007 to 2010 when they choose to use their personal savings to support Theresa—and before they can tap into the proceeds of the sale of her home. They are exceptionally fortunate that their own retirement dreams are not threatened due to their defined benefit plans and their ability to hold well-paying second career jobs upon retirement, while still receiving full pensions. They will also have income from Social Security, which they elect to defer until they can get the maximum level of payments at age 70.

However, the Life Calculator enabled the Razors to recognize the financial precipice from which they would have fallen, had Theresa lived longer than expected or had her home sold for less.

Had the Razors followed the advice in Chapter 3 urging family discussion of caregiver expenses when your parents are in their 70s, they would have been better prepared for these contingencies and would not have experienced years of economic anxiety. Fortunately, their dual second careers and decision to extend work to age 70 provided solid economic support and resulted in a comfortable retirement. Congratulations to the Razors for hard work and perseverance! You mastered Rule #3: Make Time Your Ally. Table 8.4 illustrates the timeline the Razors followed.

Table 8.4   Razors' Timeline

Date	2006–2009	2009–2015	2016–2018	2018–2021	2022–2026	2026	2032
Notable Events	James's mother diagnosed with Alzheimer's	Mother moved to nursing home	James retires at 55, begins second job Mother passes away	Nancy retires at 55, begins second job First child begins college	1st child graduates; 2nd begins college	2nd child graduates	James stops work at 70 Nancy also stops working

Fifties Decade: Maximum Earnings and Retirement Savings

Those readers entering their 50s decade are well advanced in their careers and may expect that this is the period of maximum earnings. Ironically, this is also the decade in which you are most vulnerable to job loss and to career stagnation. Many readers hit a symbolic ceiling beyond which they cannot advance in their careers. For those who are contemplating working beyond 65 or who may choose a new career direction, it is imperative that you utilize these years to gain the necessary career education and important industry contacts to make yourselves attractive to potential employers in their target industries. Please read Chapter 5 to understand strategies for new career planning.

Investment portfolios during this decade should remain broadly allocated with a continued focus on earnings, recognizing the need to finance extended longevity well into the 80s or 90s. However, those approaching the second half of this decade should consider balancing return on investments with risk management to protect against possible loss of principal that cannot be replaced, given your age.

Equally as important as return on investment is the full funding of retirement benefits. You should perform a pension audit. If a gap is revealed between the expected savings and funding level of the pension program, you should contact your retirement plan administrator to understand the expected future status of such underfunding.

On the personal front, many of you in this stage of life will experience an *Empty Nester* period as your children graduate from high school and college, though it is increasingly likely that they may return home. With this major expense behind, you will have further opportunity to increase your retirement savings, and you should begin to review your plans for the possible sale of your home. For those of you intending to downsize, it is wise to remember that timing the sale of your home to maximize price may require patience, due to the cyclical nature of the real estate market.

Fifties Profiles

*The Apples: Marketing Professionals—Rebuilding Finances
after Poor Life Decisions*

Before Divorce/After Divorce

- Dan and Sharon Apple/Dan and Christina Apple: New York City
- Ages 52 and 50/ages 53 and 35
- Dan earns $225,000, Sharon earns $90,000, Christina earns $42,000
- Teenagers, 13 and 14; two young children with Christina
- Savings of $950,000/$500,000
- Challenges:
  - Divorce and custody costs
  - Remarriage and new family
  - Investment losses
  - Career education for Christina

The Apples are a professional couple living in New York. Dan Apple is an executive at an advertising agency, earning $225,000 annually. Sharon Apple is a college professor, earning $90,000. Together, they had an after-tax income of $238,500 and two teenage children, 13 and 14 years old. They spend $210,000 annually and place the rest in their savings.

Despite the high cost of living, the couple managed their finances wisely. After years of hard work, the Apples had assets of $950,000. They estimated that by retirement, they would have saved $2.5 million at a 6 percent rate of return. Adding the value of their home, their assets should have lasted them for the rest of their lifetime, if they had continued their current pattern of spending.

Unfortunately, Dan had an affair with his office secretary, Christina. When Sharon learned of the relationship, she immediately filed for divorce. The family's assets were split. The family home was sold, and Dan used the proceeds as the down payment toward the purchase of another home, moving in with Christina, whom he married and was pregnant. Child support, tuition sharing through college for his two teenagers, a new home mortgage, and a new baby put huge financial pressures on Dan. His lifestyle has suddenly become very expensive—his expenses of $210,000 a year are now greater than the net earnings from his salary.

Using the Life Calculator, Dan learns that he will have only $262,000 at retirement remaining from his divorce settlement of $475,000. Dan is drawing down on his savings to supplement the difference between his annual living costs and his income. His savings will be exhausted immediately after he retires, even accounting for Social Security. Desperate to regain additional savings, he decides to place some of his savings into a hedge fund.

Dan, now 54, quickly suffers investment losses of $50,000 through the hedge fund. He returns to the Life Calculator and inputs the losses. The results are bleak. His remaining money will provide only one year of retirement support and will be depleted by age 65. It is with mixed feelings that Dan receives the news that he will soon again become the father of a second child by Christina.

Chagrined by his investment losses, Dan takes his money out of that risky investment vehicle and, guided by the Life Calculator, decides to cut annual costs to $160,000 and work until age 70. He figures he will be able to accumulate $1.4 million by retirement, which would last him until age 84—a good first step toward retirement security—if he had no responsibilities to his second family for college education. His first of two children from the second marriage will be entering college when Dan is 71 and his second child when he is 73. How will Dan assist their college educations? He is unable to budget any funding for either child and still have a comfortable retirement.

The Life Calculator confirms that a second income is required to finance their children's college education. Dan suggests to Christina that she plan to return to work to finance their children's educations when their younger child enter school and when she is 41 years old.

Recognizing the financial imperative of their future obligations, Christina reads about growth industries in Chapter 5 and commits to completing a college degree at night, with a career objective of

Table 8.5   The Apples' Timeline

Date	2006	2007–2011	2012–2023	2024	2025–2035	2036
Notable Events	Divorce assets divided	Investment losses $100,000	Christina has new job	Dan retires	Two children's college	Christina retires

working as a clinical technician for one of the many biopharmaceutical firms located in the region. Biotechnology is a strong growth industry where positions pay well, have structured hours and generous benefits, and pay $40,000 for beginning salaries. Christina assumes she will have steady income growth as her tenure in the industry continues.

The Apples have proven the importance of early decision making, which allowed for Christina to train for a career. If Christina decides to retire at age 65, her late career and income growth enables the family to extend their resources until she is 88. This was the most important ingredient for their financial security. Congratulations, Apples, for successfully following Rule #1: Own Your Future. Table 8.5 presents their timeline.

The Palms: Programmer—Outsourced Industry Leads to Unemployment and a Second Career

- Cindy and Jack Palm: San Mateo, California
- Ages 56 and 49
- Jack initially earned $250,000; now earns $160,000
- Children 10, 14, and 17
- Savings of $1 million
- Challenges:
  - Job loss
  - Unemployment for one year, limited employment for two years
  - College expenses

Jack Palm has often joked that the inventor of the Palm Pilot got the idea from him at his software company's dinner party 15 years ago. Whether true or not, this computer programmer was one of the first to embrace personal computers, recognizing their potential 30 years ago and surfing his company's IPO to a comfortable living in Silicon Valley.

Jack commutes 10 minutes to work every day as a veteran project manager for a software company earning $250,000 annually, plus stock options. When people have asked him why he doesn't become a CEO, he replies that he's already earning as much as they do, while still doing what he loves—programming. His 49-year-old wife, Cindy, is an active, stay-at-home mom, caring for their three children, ages 10, 14, and 17.

The Palms have an expensive lifestyle in a high-cost region of the country. Two of the children attend private school with $40,000 tuition bills. The mortgage and maintenance on their $3.64 million home in San Mateo; two foreign cars; summer camps and institutes for their children; and yearly family ski and summer vacations quickly absorb their available income. Jack and Cindy decided to fund their children's annual tuition from their savings account, as they value the small class sizes and the enriched environment at the private schools their children attend.

The Palms, like many California families, have benefited from the rapid appreciation of their residential property over the past 20 years. Such home equity is not liquid until they sell their property and downsize to a less expensive area.

The Palms' diversified portfolio is currently valued at $1.5 million, initially funded by the sale of Jack's shares in an IPO of a start-up company when he was younger and stock options from his current employer, who recently went public. Given the Palms' expensive lifestyle, they have not committed to a savings plan beyond his stock option investments, believing that his income would be sufficient to fund any future requirements. Assuming $2.2 million to $2.8 million in net proceeds from the sale of their home several years into the future after capital gains taxes, broker fees, and expenses, the Palms would expect over $5.3 million in combined home and portfolio equity by the end of the decade.

Jack's bubble bursts when he is informed that his employer intends to sell the company and his job is being restructured to a much lower position now held by a mid-level employee. Jack is offered a consulting contract for four months with continuing healthcare benefits.

The Palms at first remain unconcerned, certain that Jack will quickly identify an equally attractive position in Silicon Valley, using his many Rolodex contacts. They are committed to staying in their home, insuring their children's continuity in school and remaining close to their friends and families. Despite calling his universe of friends and business colleagues, sending out dozens of resumes, and suffering through interviews for positions that paid less and provided no stimulation, Jack is not offered any opportunity in the region, though there are positions in the Boston and New York areas.

The Palms decline to relocate. They turn to the Life Calculator to review the seriousness of their financial situation and to measure the financial benefits of various alternatives. Using the Life Calculator, they view the financial damage to their bottom line from Jack's first year of unemployment. They have drawn down $180,000 in savings to continue paying their expenses, willing to moderate their expenditures only slightly.

Beginning next year, tuition expenses will increase by a third, as their youngest child enters private school and their oldest child enrolls in a private college. The Palms will have 12 straight years of private college expenses to educate all three of their children at $40,000 a year. This is in addition to their private high school tuitions.

Jack continues to search for job opportunities and finally, after two years of unemployment, lands a federal contract as a technology consultant at $142,000, earning an after-tax income of $110,000 for a year and drawing down on his savings to support the additional family expenses. By the end of the first three years following his job loss, the Palms have depleted $430,000 in savings to maintain their current lifestyle.

Just as the panic sets in, good news arrives: The contractual arrangement leads to a higher-paying private-sector salary as Vice President of Technology at $200,000 in year four. Although it does not fully replace his $250,000 former salary, the Palms are

Table 8.6 The Palms' Timeline

Date	2006	2007–2009	2010–2013	2014–2017	2018	2019
Notable Events	Jack's job loss Youngest child starts private school	New job Oldest child starts college	Second child begins college	Second child graduates Youngest begins college	Youngest graduates	Jack retires

deeply relieved that the financial bleeding has been substantially halted.

When the Palms rerun the Life Calculator, factoring in these new developments, they decide that Jack should work to 70 to replace their lost savings and to finance the final years of their children's education. Jack will be 68 when his youngest child graduates from college. The Palms will have $1.4 million in their investment portfolio at the time of Jack's retirement. They will have greater flexibility in planning the next cycle of their lives, including deciding when to sell their large home and either downsizing or relocating to a less expensive community.

The appreciation from the sale of their home, Jack's stock options, together with their Social Security and investment income will provide the sufficient assets to support a comfortable retirement lifestyle. The Palms, despite a tough decade of lowered employment and financial exposure, reorganize their finances for a firm foundation to support themselves into their 90s. Congratulations, Palms for implementing Rule #4: Master Change! (See Table 8.6.)

Router—Real Estate Appraiser Recovering from Investment Losses and Unfunded surgery

- Eric Router: Portland, Oregon
- Age 50, single
- Earns $100,000
- Investments: $850,000
- Challenges:

- ◆ Real estate investment losses
- ◆ Litigation costs with tenants
- ◆ Minimal health insurance

Eric Router is a perpetual optimist who has been blessed with superior athletic skills, a high level of energy, and an outstanding ability to network. An aggressive rock climber and a championship skier on the University of Oregon's nationally respected ski team, he qualified for the U.S Olympic ski team, only to suffer an unfortunate injury while in training. Despite this setback, Eric continued networking in his skiing community and, soon after graduation from college, established a ski shop with a group of friends, investing his savings earned from his many years as a private ski instructor.

Eric struggled to make the business profitable and to expand its product line in the off-season. He recognized its limitations, sold his interest, and became associated with a real estate brokerage firm in the resort community. After several seasons selling resort properties, Eric decided to pursue real estate as a lifetime career and enrolled in real estate appraisal courses to receive his license. When he was notified of an employment opportunity at a large real estate company based in Portland, he applied and was hired.

Moving to Portland, Eric became active in the arts community and passionate about his new hobby of real estate investing. He was able to receive many solid tips regarding underpriced properties and began investing small amounts, initially in foreclosed properties and eventually in subprime mortgages. Trading appreciated smaller properties for larger buildings, he was able to quickly grow his wealth.

Eric purchased a home, which he substantially renovated and filled with interesting art objects. He believes he has achieved his life goals: financial security, a well-balanced lifestyle with many friends, flexible work arrangements, and the opportunity to pursue his art and athletic interests. Given his confidence in his investing abilities, Eric was indifferent about his need for risk management.

Three incidents over a period of 18 months quickly changed Eric's outlook on the need to be proactive in reducing risks. While mountain climbing with friends, Eric sustained a serious back injury, falling some distance when his rope broke. Fortunately he landed in heavy underbrush, which prevented more critical injuries. Eric's HMO financed only a minimal level of care. He was personally responsible for over $100,000 in bills for follow-up specialist care, secondary surgeries, and months of physical therapy. This, and the older skiing injury, cost Eric out-of-pocket health expenses of $128,000 for this year.

Coinciding with his physical challenge, Eric received a letter from the Oregon State Department of Transportation, written in a typical bureaucratic style, informing him that several of his multifamily properties were in the path of a proposed "Kiss & Ride" facility for the expansion of the Portland Metropolitan Express light-rail system. Eric is enraged. He had been assured, after a careful review of public records, by senior departmental officials, that they had no intent on expanding the rail facility at the time he purchased his properties. The state is willing to pay "fair-market value" for his real estate, but such values do not begin to reflect the substantial appreciation that Eric had anticipated would occur when he purchased the properties, nor the significant property improvements he had made assuming that he could amortize such costs over many years of ownership and would be receiving rent equivalent to the improved state of the properties. Eric would fail to achieve his investment goals. He would have purchased alternative properties had he been aware of this outcome.

A group of tenants in another of Eric's properties, a multifamily project, file a lawsuit against Eric for damage to their personal property resulting from water damage due to leaky windows, doors, and roofs from a major rainstorm. Eric's property insurance had an upper limit, and, given the contested nature of the legal proceedings, Eric was exposed to paying a out-of-pocket settlement of $80,000 to placate the dozen tenants whose expensive clothing, rugs, and furnishings were damaged.

Eric was referred to the LifeCalculator.Net Web site by a friend. Since using the service, he has taken actions to protect against downside risk. He purchased a more comprehensive healthcare policy, increased his property insurance on all of his real estate investments, and diversified his asset strategy.

Eric recognizes that his investment portfolio is overweight in real estate and that, given his age, he should have a broader investment matrix, which protects against inflation and market volatility. He consults the Life Calculator "Investments" tab and proceeds to sell some of his properties to achieve greater investment diversity.

Congratulations, Eric, for educating yourself on this important Rule #2: Focus on Reducing Risk. (See Table 8.7.)

Table 8.7   Eric Router's Timeline

Date	1979–1981	1981–1983	1983–1995	1995—2006	2007	2010
Notable Events	Eric graduates from college Establishes ski shop	Sells ski shop interest Begins to sell real estate Becomes a licensed real estate appraiser	Moves to Portland, OR Invests in foreclosures and sub-prime mortgages Purchases home	Begins working independently	Realizes importance of Insurance	Retires

CHAPTER 9

Join the Sixties and Seventies:
A Successful and Safe Life

The Life Calculator is a powerful tool to support lifelong financial planning. Its ability to anticipate and measure the effects of life's many changes enables you to address the variables of real life and project a realistic picture of your future.

Although I urge you to use the Life Calculator to create an initial personal profile, I think it is equally educational to read the life profiles of hypothetical families and individuals whose life experiences may mirror your own. Reading their responses to financial challenges may provide meaningful direction in your own life. All the financial analysis in the profiles is provided courtesy of the Life Calculator.

The profiles in the previous chapter and the profiles that follow, which portray an individual and couples at a specific point in their life journey, incorporate the adverse events and opportunities that have or will occur, the financial impacts of these events, and the actions taken by the hypothetical individual or couple to mitigate their results.

Sixties Decade: Transitioning into a Second Career

The decade of the 60s has become a life cycle of extended work, second careers, and active care of parents. Many of you will choose to work beyond the traditional retirement age of 65, working to 70 and beyond. It is advisable to delay drawing down on Social Security. Refer to the "Retirement Resources" tab in the Life Calculator to realize the financial advantages of delaying Social Security payments and gaining the value of future increased monthly income that might be essential later in life.

This is the decade where balance between career and family takes an ironic twist, with most readers electing to emphasize the care of aging parents and involvement with young grandchildren. If selecting a second career, it is advisable that such employment begin early during this decade to enable the employee to gain the benefit of any potential employer-matched contributions and to reduce the likelihood of age bias.

Volunteer work and active involvement in personal hobbies consume increasing amounts of your time during this decade. It is important that you develop those interests and relationships, if you are to have a comfortable network of opportunities and friendships when you retire.

Investment portfolios during this decade should be transitioned to lower-risk products including money market funds, CDs, and Treasury inflation-protected securities (TIPS). Avoid the temptation of garnering small marginal increases in investment returns by buying lower-quality securities and/or CDs. Your investment objective must be risk management. Any investment losses sustained during this decade will not be recovered in future years.

Sale of your home and a decision regarding where you will eventually retire should be addressed during this decade, if not already determined. Read the extended discussion regarding housing alternatives in preparing a sequential plan for future housing requirements, recognizing that for most readers, nursing or dependent care will be necessary. Real estate markets are highly cyclical, and the ability to maximize sales price at the top of the market and/or to buy at the bottom end of a market downturn requires careful planning, market education, and generally the involvement of a well-respected broker.

Sixties Profiles

Dell: Single-Parent Nurse with Good Benefits, Secure Retirement

- Adriana Dell: Orlando, Florida
- Divorced nurse earning $60,000
- Age 61
- One child
- Savings of $100,000
- The challenges:
  - ◆ Divorce
  - ◆ Low savings rate
  - ◆ Small investment portfolio

Adriana Dell is energized. A 61-year-old operating room nurse from Orlando, Florida, she has just participated in a five-hour surgery that saved the life of a gunshot victim. With days like this, she feels full of enthusiasm and can't imagine why she should retire at 65. Surely life at retirement couldn't be any better than this.

Ten years ago, Adriana underwent a messy divorce. Left with only $100,000 in assets coming from the sale of her home and only saving $3,000 annually, she wondered how she would be able to save sufficient resources to finance her retirement on her after-tax salary of $52,000. If she retired at 65 and didn't cut her annual spending of $49,000, her meager savings would only compound to $269,000 with a 6 percent rate of return. Even with Social Security, her retirement assets would be depleted in her mid-70s.

Adriana considered her employment options. Fortunately, she was able to secure a new job that had an employer-matched 401(k) retirement plan, thus enhancing the value of her $3,000 a year savings to double that amount. Adriana's employment in the healthcare industry alleviated one of the largest potential hazards to her retirement account—unfunded healthcare costs.

Her concern regarding funding her son's college expenses was also resolved when her son received an ROTC scholarship paying for his entire college tuition. Now, at age 65, she has a projected $326,000 in assets, that with Social Security should last until age 81.

Adriana knows she is likely to live well into her 90s, as she is healthy, has no family history of health issues, and her own mother is still alive and active at 90. Her mother has stated on many occasions that she will gift Adriana and her two other remaining daughters with her estate. Adriana does not consider it wise to plan on receiving any money, as her mother may well experience the need for expensive care in her later years.

The Life Calculator exercise on extending her employment until age 70 convinces Adriana. She is elated to find that she can extend her retirement security, even leaving an inheritance for her son, by working the additional 5 years. Adriana has always considered her home a reserve fund, which she is prepared to tap by using a reverse mortgage to fund any remaining years beyond 91 (see Chapter 6).

As a nurse and a single mom, Adriana should be proud of her accomplishments. She has achieved the retirement security that has eluded many families and individuals through her disciplined budgeting, sound career planning, and hard work. Congrats, Adriana! You prove the value of Rule #3: Make Time Your Ally.

The Blackberrys: Displaced Professionals Relocating to Secure Employment and Investing in a Personal Web-based Business

- Ken and Mary Blackberry: Houston, Texas, relocate to Austin, Texas
- Ages 60 and 54
- Ken makes $95,000, Mary makes $104,000
- Four children
- Savings of $300,000 beyond retirement accounts
- The challenges:
  - Double job loss
  - Loss of pensions

The Blackberrys are professionals in the financial services industry. Ken Blackberry now works as a financial consultant to state and local governments in the energy sector and has been appointed as an adjunct professor, in the graduate business school of the University of Texas–Austin. Mary Blackberry works as a CPA for a state agency. They relocated to Austin from Houston in 2002, where they both had been employed for over 15 years.

Both previously worked at Enron Corporation, Mary in the tax department and Ken in governmental relations. They are among the thousands of employees whose lives have been negatively affected by the financial mismanagement of the company. The Blackberrys enjoyed their professional careers while at Enron, earning good salaries and investing their 401(k)s in company stock, certain that Enron would continue to prosper.

Both had been divorced at the time of their introduction 15 years ago and came into their marriage with limited assets, each with two young children and a strong commitment to creating financial security for themselves and educational opportunities for their children. Their merged family lived a comfortable life in Houston on their combined salaries of $250,000. Two of their four children have graduated from private universities and two are currently attending public college. The Blackberrys had never seriously budgeted, believing that their future income and retirement were secure. Once they had educated their children, they plan to begin setting aside more savings.

After the collapse of Enron, Ken and Mary realized that they had been hit by an economic tsunami: They had both lost their jobs; their pensions were devalued to less than $5,000; they owned a home in a community where there were more for-sale signs than stop signs; and they would need to buy an expensive plan to extend their healthcare insurance. Unlike many of their Enron colleagues, the Blackberrys realized that the good times were over, and they quickly moved to find jobs in the public sector where they could be assured of pensions and benefits.

The Blackberrys were fortunate. Mary's CPA was in demand in both public and private sectors, but she elected the security of a state job. Ken had served as a government liaison for Enron throughout Texas and the Southwest and was well respected by many government officials. He had been previously appointed as a lecturer at the business school, ironically teaching corporate governance.

Using the Life Calculator, they mapped out their future strategy. They were among the first to sell their large home, buying a much smaller townhouse in less-expensive Austin, the state's capital and the location of the main campus of the University of Texas. The appreciated $500,000 savings from their home sale was allocated to a sound investment portfolio, earning an average of 6 percent annually. Together with the $300,000 they had built up by investing outside their Enron 401(k), the Blackberrys have the foundation for building a new retirement nest egg.

Mary is enrolled in a defined-benefit plan at the state tax agency that will, at her retirement after 16 years at age 70, pay her 50 percent of her last salary, which she estimates will be roughly $135,000, escalating from her original $104,000 salary base. That $67,600, combined with their joint Social Security payments will enable them to live comfortably in the lower-cost Austin community, enjoying the many free functions associated with the university. Ken earns $95,000 including both his university salary and consulting fee.

The Blackberrys currently spend $154,000 annually, with the remainder directed to retirement savings. While the Life Calculator indicates that Ken Blackberry should work until 70 to secure his families finances, the university has a mandatory retirement age of 65, reducing his $95,000 annual income to the $65,000 consulting fee he received. By the time Ken Blackberry retires at 70, the family will have accrued nearly $1.3 million, providing all the retirement comfort they will need into their 90s.

The Blackberrys have learned an important lesson from their Enron debacle: Anticipate that adverse events will occur in your life, ensure that you will have a reserve savings account, diversify your investments outside your employer's 401(k), and be prepared with actions to mitigate the damage. The Blackberrys have now completed an exercise reviewing the other adverse events that may still impact them: the care of her elderly parents, extended longevity, and uninsured health costs.

The Blackberrys are proactive in planning the caregiving needs of Mary's parents, who are in their late 70s. They have all discussed her parents' finances, and Ken and Mary know their preferences for care. They have certified that all health insurance and legal documents are in place. Mary's parents appear to have taken the necessary financial steps to provide for themselves, but the Blackberrys are earmarking assets in their own investment account to supplement the parents' funds, if necessary.

Mary and Ken have created a health balance sheet, have reexamined their long-term care insurance documents, and are diligent in following the prescribed nutrition and exercise program outlined by their doctors to avoid the onset of adult diabetes, which is present in both their families. They are relieved that they both have employer-provided health insurance.

Although they are still adjusting to the substantial changes in their personal and professional lives, the Blackberrys are beginning to formulate plans for third careers, as entrepreneurs in their 60s and 70s, hoping to launch their own Web-based business advising small companies that have tax issues with state and local governments. They look forward to working together and to sharing their knowledge with business owners.

The Blackberrys are confident that they will have sufficient resources to support their extended longevity while living active, stimulating lifestyles (see Table 9.1). Congratulations, Blackberrys, for serving as a model for families who have been besieged by the unsettling dynamics of corporate malfeasance! You win the award for Rule #4: Mastering Change.

Table 9.1   The Blackberrys' Timeline

	2002	2003–2011	2012–2016	2017
Notable Events	Blackberrys, ages 55 and 49, suffer job loss and move to Austin, Texas	Rebuild retirement finances	Ken retires in 2012	Mary retires

Seventies Decade: A Time of Enjoyment

By this decade the majority of you will have fully retired from your careers, but a significant percentage may still choose to be actively involved in professional pursuits—generally those who are entrepreneurs or engaged in professional services. Creating a new lifestyle to replace as much as 50 years spent actively employed is a challenge to those who have not made the effort during their 60s to engage in volunteer and community service activities. For others who have created personal interests and volunteer relationships, this decade may be one of highly active participation with crowded schedules and great enjoyment.

Health and estate planning dominate the priorities as you address any medical issues you may confront and prepare a sobering chart of future medical requirements. It is vital that you commit to a daily regimen of proper nutrition, exercise, meditation, communication with others, and learning, if you are to remain healthy. The focus on quality of life requires you to be vigilant regarding the prevention of medical problems and in developing a lifestyle that takes control of your health.

Equally important is a financial audit of your resources and expenses. Consideration of reverse mortgages, lowered budgets, and insurance support will be elements of any sound financial plan. For those of you who expect to have resources beyond that which you require under the worst-case scenario, it is valuable to engage in reviewing estate planning issues: wills, probates, taxes, and capital gains.

Seventies Profiles

The Trios: Enjoying a Delayed Retirement after Caring for Aging Parents

- Hank and Trudy Trio: Peoria, Illinois
- Ages 76 and 71
- Union workers, construction and hospitality
- Hank earns $75,000 and Trudy earns $47,000
- Five children

- Savings of $209,000
- The challenges:
  - Care for aging parents
  - Rebuilding emergency fund

Hank and Trudy Trio retired six years ago to Las Vegas, Nevada, from outside Peoria, Illinois. Hank worked for 25 years on construction projects with an average income of $65,000 a year. He was elected as a representative for his union bargaining team, the United Brotherhood of Carpenters, and eventually, became engaged in national union politics, earning $75,000 annually.

Trudy was able to work part-time in the local hotel industry, earning $20,000 a year, due to the live-in support of her mother, who helped take care of the family's five children. Once her youngest child was in high school, Trudy became involved full-time as a paid organizer for a local union group, a chapter of the Service Employees International Union (SEIU), earning $47,000 annually.

Trudy's earnings were necessary as a supplement to her husband's salary, assisting in covering household expenses and allowing the family the luxury of weekend fishing trips. They bought a Winnebago to lower the costs of food and lodging when traveling. Hank is especially proud of their five-bedroom home, which he had built using his expertise in construction. When Trudy began working full-time, they committed to saving $300 a month, $3,600 a year. Prior to her working, they were able to save less than $1,500 a year.

When Hank was 57, the Trios used the Life Calculator, which estimated that, with their savings of $209,000 and a return of 6 percent, they should be able to amass $369,400 by the time Hank retired at 65. This sum should protect, in addition to their pension and Social Security payments, against any adverse events. The Trios, having worked hard all their life, would like to increase their spending by 20 percent during retirement.

The Trios valued the strong benefit package offered by their employers. Trudy and two of their children are diabetic, and their healthcare program covered most medical expenses. With her and her husband's union pensions, which provide them with the equivalent of 60 percent of their salaries, plus two Social Security incomes, the Trios believed that they would have a secure retirement.

The Trios appear to have managed their family finances effectively. They did not have to pay for their children's college tuitions, as three of their children attended public universities financed through a 529 plan funded by their grandmother, while the other two children pursued technical fields, living at home and using a combination of loans and part-time jobs to cover tuition expenses. Trudy's mother, in addition to funding her grandchildren's education, had wisely purchased healthcare and long-term care insurance while in her 50s, with the objective of not becoming a burden to her family.

Unfortunately, Hank's parents had not proved as successful in their financial planning. Their retirement assets were depleted when they were in their early 70s. The senior Trios had determined not to buy long-term care insurance, expecting that the proceeds from the profits from their business would be sufficient to fund any medical expenses. Both Trios suffered serious illnesses. Hank Sr. developed Alzheimer's in his early 70s, and his wife was diagnosed with diabetes. They initially lived at an expensive assisted-living facility, but after several years, they were unable to afford the escalating costs. Hank and Trudy, by this time 59 and 54 years old, were the only family members in a position to contribute financially, and they felt obligated to offer support.

Hank and Trudy realized that contributing to the support of his parents' $145,000 annual nursing home bill was not realistic, as it would quickly deplete their savings. It was cheaper to move Hank's parents into their home rather than pay for a nursing home, now that their children had grown and they had room in their home.

The Trios hired two caregivers, who provided round-the-clock support for all three parents, including Trudy's mother, who had become increasingly infirm. Even with Medicare support for the parents, the Trios would need to make an annual contribution of

$40,000, as well as pay $55,000 to renovate their home for elderly access, upgrade the bathrooms, and add a bedroom. They were able to sell his parents' home and net $127,000 after expenses to assist in financing the costs of their care.

Not knowing how many years they would be financing care, Trudy and Hank realized that their dream of retiring early and relocating to Nevada was impossible. Realizing their personal savings account could conceivably be entirely depleted, depending on the number of years that they cared for their parents, the Trios inputted the new information into the Life Calculator and were alarmed by the numbers. Six years of support for their parents, even with the sale of their parents' home, would reduce their savings account to $59,700 at Hank's retirement, which would run out when they were in their 70s.

The Trios decided that they should extend their employment as long as possible, since they were unable to relocate and needed the additional income. They determined, after running the numbers in the Life Calculator, to extend their employment five years, to age 70 for Hank and age 67 for Trudy, to afford the cost of caring for their aging parents.

Working these extra years, the Trios rebuilt their depleted retirement account back to $122,110 at Trudy's retirement, which, combined with the sale of their home at $500,000, would be sufficient for their retirement, if they did not suffer any adverse events. Given Trudy's diabetes, the Trios were concerned that she might experience a health incident that was not covered completely by their insurance. With their limited savings, the Trios are entirely dependent on Social Security and their pensions to finance their retirement. Fortunately, their delayed retirement ages have increased their Social Security payments by 71 percent for Hank and 42 percent for Trudy, while allowing them to achieve their increased retirement spending.

After the last of their parents died seven years ago, the Trios sold their home and moved to Lake Havasu to be near their children, grandchildren, and great-grandchildren. They enjoy the climate and recreational activities and are secure in knowing that,

Table 9.2   The Trios' Timeline

Date	1986–1987	1988–1994	1995	1996–1999	2000	2002
Notable Events	Trios, ages 57 and 52, plan to retire at 65 and 62	Care of aging parents Decide to work to 70 and 67	Trios, ages 66 and 61 Parents pass away	Rebuild retirement accounts	Hank retires at age 70	Trudy retires at age 67

with their extended employment and double pensions, they will not be a burden on their family, even if they live to their mid-90s. Congratulations for achieving Rule #1: Owning Your Future. (See Table 9.2.)

The Motos: Seniors Giving Back to Society with Volunteer Service

- Peter and Betty Moto: Minneapolis, Minnesota
- Ages 76 and 75
- Income of $200,000
- Four children
- Savings of $950,000
- The challenges:
  - Three years of hospital and rehabilitation expenses for an injured uninsured son
  - Savings reduced by $500,000

Peter and Betty Moto from Minneapolis, Minnesota, ages 76 and 75, have achieved their retirement dream, although it was delayed by four years. They finally relocated to Sedona, Arizona, two years ago, often described as a breathtakingly beautiful countryside with massive red rock formations.

The Motos first vacationed in the region more than 30 years ago, when they attended a National Boy Scout Jamboree with their sons. Both were captivated by the beauty of the outdoors, the active art scene in Sedona, the moderate climate, and the diversity of activities. These include white-water rafting, hiking, rock climbing, and fishing. The proximity of Phoenix, Arizona, as a major metropolitan area was also a factor. They returned many times for family vacations during the summer and winter and decided over 15 years ago to seriously explore the area as a potential retirement location.

The Motos had decided that Peter would retire early—at 60, so they would be young enough to enjoy the physical activities of Arizona and able to establish themselves in the community. They both planned to volunteer—Betty in the arts community and Peter with nonprofit health groups. They recognized that moving cross-country to a community would be a difficult adjustment, so they decided that Betty should begin spending large blocks of time in Sedona to build relationships in the area. The Motos rented a home and Betty spent extensive time in Sedona, quickly becoming active in several groups and developing a circle of friends.

The Motos' dream of an early retirement was dealt a lethal blow when one of their sons, in his early 20s, became the victim of a traffic accident requiring years of recovery, physical and occupational therapy, and parental involvement in his medical care. As a young associate in a real estate brokerage firm, he had not purchased healthcare or disability coverage.

Betty returned to Minneapolis full-time to manage the medical care of her youngest son, while Peter delayed his retirement by five years. The Motos were anxious that he receive the best available medical support, and they began underwriting the uninsured costs for private rooms, specialists, and extended therapy. Their total contribution to his medical expenses is expected to be more than $500,000 in the three years of his recovery. Up until this tragic event, the Motos seemed to have managed a financially secure existence.

Betty and Peter raised their four sons on his salary as an engineer working for Medtronics Corporation in Minneapolis, where he was employed for 20 years following his earlier joint appointments in the engineering and science departments at the University of Minnesota. Betty, educated in art and archeology, had, until the birth of her second child, worked at the Walker Art Museum.

Three of their sons were very active in sports, with two sons earning college scholarships as ice hockey players. All three sons are college graduates. Their fourth son, the second oldest child, was diagnosed with a severe learning disability at an early age, required special schooling and daily tutoring. He eventually attended an expensive boarding school. He now lives in a residential community and works at a local bank.

The Motos have two retirement plans: a defined pension from the University of Minnesota, for Peter's 20-year employment as a professor, providing him with $70,000 annually after his retirement, and a 401(k) from Medtronics. These plans provide the financial support for their retirement. Peter had always contributed the maximum amount to his 401(k), with the purpose of taking early retirement at age 60 and moving to Oregon.

Peter and Betty also were conservative in their spending, investing additional monies from Peter's $200,000 Medtronics salary in a reserve savings account. They had initially created the fund, using the Life Calculator, to support three potentially adverse events:

1. Outliving their 401(k) savings due to extended longevity by either or both
2. Protecting against their uninsured healthcare costs
3. Providing a long-term financial annuity for their autistic son in residential care

Ironically, this advance planning created the financial resources they would eventually shift to fund their youngest son's medical care following his auto accident.

While working at Medtronic, Peter increased his savings to $25,000 a year out of his $150,000 after-tax income for his impending retirement. Medtronic offered him a $10,000-limit employer match, so he placed $10,000 of his savings into his matched 401(k) and the rest into his reserve fund.

After their son's accident and their decision to spend $500,000 for medical care, the Motos ran the Life Calculator to view the consequences of that expense and Peter's additional work years. The Motos realize that they will have $720,000 remaining at retirement. Though less than initially planned, they are comfortable with the financial resources of Peter's Medtronic options, worth $700,000, the

Table 9.3   The Motos' Timeline

Date	1964	1965–1973	1973–1989	1990–1993	1994
Notable Events	Motos first visit Sedona, Arizona	Motos decide to retire in Sedona	Peter begins job at Medtronics	Peter, age 60 Son is in car accident	Retire and settle in Sedona
		Start saving for early retirement	Betty stops working	Delay retirement	

sale of their Minneapolis home for $1.4 million, and their two retirement pensions.

The Motos nurtured their son back to health and moved to Sedona with him and their learning-disabled son. They can finally actualize their retirement dream.

They quickly settle into life in Sedona, since Betty had maintained her relationships through calls and e-mails during the absent four years (see Table 9.3). Congratulations, Motos, on proving the value of Rule #4: Mastering Change—you deserve to finally enjoy your retirement!

Now that you have seen how others have used the Life Calculator, it is time for you to do your first personal planning profile, if you have not already done so. Return to Chapter 3, gather the financial information you will need to input, log on to LifeCalculator.Net, and follow the prompts. The Life Calculator will take you through the process step by step.

It is advisable to create what-if scenarios for your own personal profile to anticipate the negative impact that such events may have on your finances. As have been demonstrated in these hypothetical profiles, early planning can reduce financial losses or mitigate financial damages that can occur.

Endnotes

Chapter 1

1. "In Their Dreams: What Will Boomers Inherit?" *AARP Data Digest* 139 (May 2006).

Chapter 2

1. "United States General Exit Poll," November 8, 2006. Conducted by Edison/Mitofsky. Retrieved from www.foxnews.com/projects/pdf/ushouse.pdf.
2. "Fast Facts: Life Expectancy," 2004 Data, National Center for Health Statistics, www.cdc.gov/nchs/fastats/lifexpec.htm.
3. Heidi Hartmann, "Social Security: Why Boomer Women Need More," 2006, Global Generations Policy Institute, *Harvard Generations Policy Journal* and Harvard Generations Policy Program. Retrieved from www.genpolicy.com/2006_journal/p_files/social_security.pdf.
4. "In the Middle, A Report on Multicultural Boomers Coping with Family and Aging Issues," *AARP Data Digest* (July 2001).
5. "When a Parent Moves In," *Consumer Reports* (October 2002).
6. The National Center for Assisted Living, *2000 Survey of Assisted Living Facilities.*
7. "Mom? Dad? I'm Home!" *BusinessWeek Online,* Personal Finance (June 5, 2006). Retrieved from www.businessweek.com/magazine/content/06_23/b3987116.htm.
8. "How Americans View Personal Wealth vs. How Financial Planners View This Wealth, Americans Think Wealth Is Harder for Them to Accumulate than Do Planners," Consumer Federation of America (January 9, 2006).

9. Christian Weller and Edward N. Wolff, *Retirement Income: The Crucial Role of Social Security* (Washington, D.C.: Economic Policy Institute, 2005).

10. Ruth Helman, Matthew Greenwald & Associates, Craig Copeland, and Jack VanDerhei, "Will More of Us Be Working Forever? The 2006 Retirement Confidence Survey," Employee Benefit Research Institute and Matthew Greenwald & Associates, Inc. (April 2006), www.ebri.org/publications/ib/index.cfm?fa=ibDisp&content_id=3630.

11. "Slow-but-Steady Wins: Regular 401(k) Savers Overcome Bear Market," Employee Benefit Research institute and Investment Company Institute, press release describing 401(k) Plan Asset Allocation, Account Balances, and Loan Activity in 2005 (August 2006).

12. "2007 Social Security Changes" (October 2006), Social Security Administration, www.ssa.gov/pressoffice/colafacts.htm, individual benefits for a couple, both receiving benefits.

13. "National Compensation Survey: Employee Benefits in Private Industry in the United States, March 2006," U.S Bureau of Labor Statistics (August 2006).

14. "America's Small Businesses Failing to Meet Retirement Needs of Their Owners and Employees According to Nationwide Survey," Press Release of Survey conducted by Harris Interactive/ShareBuilder 401(k), November 13, 2006.

15. Ibid.

16. Benjamin Yang, Julia Bonafede, and Steven Foresti, "2005 Wilshire Report on Corporate Pension Funding Levels (FASB 87), Wilshire Associates (May 13, 2005). Retrieved from www.wilshire.com/Company/2005_Corporate_Funding_Report.pdf.

17. Social Security Administration, *Fast Facts & Figures about Social Security, 2006* (Washington, D.C.: U.S. Government Printing Office, 2006).

18. Sunwha Lee and Lois Shaw, "Gender and Economic Security in Retirement," Institute for Women's Policy Research (2003). Retrieved from www.iwpr.org/pdf/D456.pdf.

19. Social Security Administration, *Fast Facts & Figures about Social Security, 2006.*

20. Lee and Shaw, "Gender and Economic Security in Retirement."

21. "Wiser Special Report: The Pay Gap's Connected to The Retirement Gap," Women's Institute for a Secure Retirement

(WISER) http://216.70.87.179/portal/index.php?option=com_content&task=view&id=188&Itemid=0, www.wiser.heinz.org.

22. "As Retirement Lifestyle Expectations Fall, Savings Stress Rises," Mercer Human Resource Consulting (October 30, 2006). Retrieved from www.mercerhr.com/pressrelease/details.jhtml/dynamic/idContent/1247510.

Chapter 4

1. Lisa Clemans-Cope, Bowen Garrett, and Catherine Hoffman, "Changes in Employee's Health Insurance Coverage, 2001–2005," Kaiser Commission on Medicaid and the Uninsured (October 2006). Retrieved from www.kff.org/uninsured/upload/7570.pdf.

2. Paul Fronstin, "Savings Needed to Fund Health Insurance and Health Care Expenses in Retirement," Issue Brief No. 295, EBRI (July 2006). Retrieved from www.ebri.org/pdf/briefspdf/EBRI_IB_07-20061.pdf.

3. The National Center for Assisted Living, 2000 Survey of Assisted Living Facilities.

4. Jack VanDerhei, "Defined Benefit Plan Freezes: Who's Affected, How Much, and Replacing Lost Accruals," Issue Brief No. 291, Employee Benefit Research Institute (EBRI) (March 2006), www.iscebs.org/PDF/EBRI_1.pdf.

5. Ibid.

6. "Job Openings and Labor Turnover Survey 2005," Bureau of Labor Statistics, Retrieved from www.bls.gov/news.release/jolts.toc.htm.

7. Ibid.

8. Erika Steinmetz, U.S. Census Bureau, Americans with Disabilities: 2002, "Prevalence of Disability," June–September 2002, Survey of Income and Program Participation (May 2006). Retrieved from www.census.gov/prod/2006pubs/p70-107.pdf.

9. "Trends in Longevity and Retirement Planning, 2003 TIAA Mortality Table," *TIAA-Cref Quarterly* (Summer 2003).

10. Ruth Helman et al., "Will More of Us Be Working Forever?" EBRI, Issue Brief No. 292 (April 2006). Assumes uncovered expenses of $30,000/year for 10 years. The average worker expects to spend 20 years in retirement. Retrieved from www.ebri.org/pdf/EBRI_IB_04-2006_1.pdf.

11. E. Mavis Hetherington, "Marriage and Divorce American Style," *The American Prospect* (April 8, 2002).

12. Lynn Gottschalk, "The Impact of Divorce on Retirement Decisions," (April 2006), Federal Trade Commission. Retrieved from http://client.norc.org/jole/SOLEweb/Gottschalk.pdf.

13. National Partnership for Women and Families "Family Leave Benefits: Essential to Seniors Receiving the Care They Need," 2002.

14. Jonathan Clements, "Long-Term Care Planning: How to Protect Against the High Cost of Nursing Homes," *The Wall Street Journal* (February 22, 2006), p. D1.

15. U.S. Census Bureau, "2005 American Community Survey: S1401 School Enrollment." Retrieved from http://factfinder.census.gov/servlet/STTable?_bm=y&-geo_id=01000US&-qr_name=ACS_2005_ESTG00_S1401&-ds_name=ACS_2005_EST_G00.

16. "Trends in College Pricing 2004," The College Board, www.collegeboard.com.

17. Health Care Costs Survey, Aug. 2005.

18. "Employer Health Benefits, 2006 Summary of Findings," Kaiser Family Foundation and Health Research and Educational Trust, p. 2. Retrieved from www.kff.org/insurance/7527/upload/7528.pdf.

19. "Fidelity Estimates $200,000 Now Needed to Cover Retiree Health Care Costs," March 6, 2006, News Release by Fidelity Investments, http://content.members.fidelity.com/Inside_Fidelity/fullStory/1,,6605,00.html.

20. "Employer Health Benefits, 2006 Annual Survey."

21. "Trends in Longevity and Retirement Planning."

22. Paul Fronstin, "Savings Needed to Fund Health Insurance and Health Care Expenses in Retirement," Issue Brief No. 295, EBRI (July 2006).

23. "Employer Health Benefits, 2006 Annual Survey," Kaiser Family Foundation and Health Research and Educational Trust, Calculated using annual data 1999–2005.

24. "Assisted Living Resident Profile," National Center for Assisted Living, www.ncal.org/about/resident.htm. Last accessed December 9, 2006.

25. Peter Kemper, Harriet Komisar, and Lisa Alecxih, "Long-Term Care over an Uncertain Future: What Can Current Retirees Expect?" *Inquiry*, vol. 42, no. 4 (Winter 2005/2006), pp. 335–350.

26. "Genworth Financial 2006 Cost of Care Survey," (March 2006). Retrieved from www.aahsa.org/advocacy/assisted_living/reports_data/documents/Genworth_cost_study.pdf.

27. "Assisted Living Resident Profile." Statistics compiled from several different sources.

28. Kemper, Komisar, and Alecxih, "Long-Term Care over an Uncertain Future."

29. "Assisted Living Resident Profile."

30. "The Metlife Market Survey of Nursing Home and Home Care Costs," Metlife (September 2006). Retrieved from www.metlife.com/WPSAssets/18756958281159455975V1F2006NHHCMarketSurvey.pdf.

31. Kemper, Komisar, and Alecxih, "Long-Term Care over an Uncertain Future."

32. "Will More of Us Be Working Forever? The 2006 Retirement Confidence Survey" (April 2006), Employee Benefit Research Institute and Matthew Greenwald & Associates, Inc.

33. "Slow-but-Steady Wins: Regular 401(k) Savers Overcome Bear Market," Employee Benefit Research Institute and Investment Company Institute, press release describing 401(k) Plan Asset Allocation, Account Balances, and Loan Activity in 2005 (August 2006).

34. Yang, Bonafede, and Foresti, "2005 Wilshire Report on Corporate Pension Funding Levels."

35. Diane E. Lewis, "Survey Notes Disparity in Search by Age Group," *The Boston Globe*, Out in The Field, citing a survey by DBM (May 25, 2003).

36. Proctor DeNavas-Walt and Lee, "Income, Poverty, and Health Insurance Coverage in the United States: 2005," U.S. Census Bureau, Current Population Reports (August 2006).

37. "Job Openings and Labor Turnover Survey 2005," Bureau of Labor Statistics.

38. Lewis, "Survey Notes Disparity."

39. U.S. Census Bureau, "Prevalence of Disability."

40. A. M. Miniño, M. Heron, and B. L. Smith, "Deaths: Preliminary Data for 2004," *Health E-Stats* (April 19, 2006). Retrieved from www.cdc.gov/nchs/products/pubs/pubd/hestats/prelimdeaths04/preliminarydeaths04.htm.

41. "Trends in Longevity and Retirement Planning."

42. "Making Your Money Last for a Lifetime: Why You Need to Know about Annuities," 2003, WISER and The Actuarial Foundation. Retrieved from www.actuarialfoundation.org/consumer/Wiser_annuities.pdf.
43. Hartmann, "Social Security: Why Boomer Women Need More."
44. "Fertility, Family Planning and Reproductive Health of U.S. Women: Data from the 2002 National Survey of Family Growth," *Vital and Health Statistics,* series 23, no. 25 (December 2005).
45. Susan Stewart, Wendy Manning, and Pamela Smock, "Union Formation among Men in the U.S.: Does Having Prior Children Matter?" *Journal of Marriage and the Family,* vol. 65, no. 1 (2003): 90–104.
46. www.divorcestatistics.org, citing Jennifer Baker, Forest Institute of Professional Psychology, Springfield. Last accessed April 6, 2007.
47. Gottschalk, "The Impact of Divorce on Retirement Decisions."
48. Steven J. Haider, Alison Jacknowitz, and Robert F. Schoeni, "The Economic Status of Elderly Divorced Women," Michigan Retirement Research Center, Working Paper WP 2003-046 (2003).
49. "In the Middle, A Report on Multicultural Boomers Coping with Family and Aging Issues," *AARP Data Digest* (July 2001).
50. National Partnership for Women and Families, "Family Leave Benefits."
51. "When a Parent Moves In," *Consumer Reports 2002* (October 2002).
52. National Alliance for Caregiving and AARP, "Caregiving in the U.S," (April 2004). Retrieved from www.caregiving.org/data/04finalreport.pdf.
53. The National Center for Assisted Living, 2000 Survey of Assisted Living Facilities.
54. U.S. Census Bureau, "2005 American Community Survey: S1401 School Enrollment." Retrieved from http://factfinder.census.gov/servlet/STTable?_bm=y&-geo_id=01000US&-qr_name=ACS_2005_EST_G00_S1401&-ds_name=ACS_2005_EST_G00.
55. "Trends in College Pricing 2004."
56. InflationData.com, http://inflationdata.com/Inflation/Inflation_Rate/CurrentInflation.asp, Last accessed September 16, 2006.

57. "In Their Dreams: What Will Boomers Inherit?" *AARP Data Digest* 139 (May 2006).
58. Ibid.
59. Ibid.

Chapter 5

1. Bureau of Labor Statistics, "Number of Jobs Held in a Lifetime," U.S. Dept. of Labor, Frequently Asked Questions. Retrieved from www.bls.gov/nls/nlsfaqs.htm#anch41.
2. Thomas C. Nelson, "Creating Jobs in the 21st Century: The Business Case for Workers Age 50+: A Good Investment," *AARP Data Digest* (May 2006).
3. "Trends in Longevity and Retirement Planning."
4. Social Security Administration, "Find Your Retirement Age," www.ssa.gov/retirechartred.htm. Last accessed February 5, 2007.
5. Social Security Administration, "Delayed Retirement Credits," www.ssa.gov/retire2/delayret.htm. Last accessed February 5, 2007.
6. "Turning Boomers into Boomerangs," *The Economist* (Feb. 16, 2006).
7. Barbara A. Butrica, Smith Karen, and C. Eugene Steuerle, "Working for a Good Retirement," Center for Retirement Research at Boston College (March 2006).
8. "The New Retirement Survey From Merrill Lynch Reveals How Baby Boomers Will Transform Retirement," Merrill Lynch Press Releases (February 22, 2005). Retrieved from www.ml.com/?id=7695_7696_8149_46028_46503_46635.
9. Bureau of Labor Statistics, "Jobs Most Affected by Baby-boomer Retirements," U.S. Dept of Labor, Employment Projections. Retrieved from www.bls.gov/opub/ted/2000/Aug/wk4/art04.htm.
10. Bureau of Labor Statistics, "National Compensation Survey: Employee Benefits in Private Industry in the U.S.," U.S. Department of Labor (March 2006).
11. "Employer Health Benefits, 2006 Annual Survey," Kaiser Family Foundation and Health Research & Educational Trust. Retrieved from www.kff.org/insurance/7527/upload/7527.pdf.
12. Emily Brandon and James M. Pethoukoukis, "Going Your Own Way," *U.S. News & World Reports* (April 3, 2006).
13. Lawrence M. Fisher, "More Retirees Opting to Launch Startups," *Business 2.0 Magazine* (July 5, 2006).

14. Lynn Karoly and Julie Zissimopoulos, "Self-Employment and the 50+ Population," *AARP Data Digest* (2004).

15. Mercer Human Resources, "Employee Benefits Most Generous in U.S. Government, Education, and Nonprofit Sectors" (August 29, 2005). Retrieved from www.mercerhr.com/pressrelease/details. jhtml/dynamic/idContent/1191625.

16. Deloitte & Touch, LLP, "Eye to the Future: How TMT (Technology, Media, Telecommunications) Advances Could Change the Way We Live in 2010" (March 2006). Retrieved from www. deloitte.com/dtt/cda/doc/content/UK_TMT_Eyetothefuture_06.pdf.

17. "Home and Office—Workers Want It All," Hudson Productivity Survey (July 19, 2006). Retrieved from www.rasmussenreports. com/2006/July%20Dailies/homeOffice.htm.

18. "Home Office or Corner Office?: Telecommuting Best for Staff-Level Employees, Survey Shows," *Telecommuting Journal,* citing Officeteam Survey (August 3, 2006).

19. Bureau of Labor Statistics, "American Time Use Survey 2005 Results," July 27, 2006, U.S. Department of Labor. Retrieved from www.bls.gov/news.release/pdf/atus.pdf.

20. Alex Wellen, "Degrees of Acceptance," *The New York Times* (July 30, 2006).

21. Ibid.

22. Vicki Phillips, CEO, "Online Degrees—Public Acceptance," www.GetEducated.com.

Chapter 6

1. "Don't Forget Home Equity," *BusinessWeek Online* (August 15, 2005), Personal Interview with Dr. Dean Gatzlaff. Retrieved from www.businessweek.com/magazine/content/05_33/b3947135_mz070.htm.

2. "Housing Price Index," June 1, 2006, Office of Federal Housing Enterprise Oversight. Retrieved from www.ofheo.gov/media/pdf/1q06hpi.pdf.

3. Melinda Fulmer, "Most Expensive Cities for Renters," MSN.Com (August 2006), http://realestate.msn.com/Rentals/Article. aspx?cp-documentid=797247.

4. "Behind One Gate, Two Paths," *The New York Times* (April 12, 2005).
5. Ben Brown, "Communes for Grownups: Looking for the Ideal Place to Retire? Create It Yourself," *AARP Bulletin* (November 2004).
6. Jane Goss, "Aging at Home: For a Lucky Few, A Wish Come True," *The New York Times* (February 9, 2006).
7. "The Village Concept: A Founder's Manual: How to Make Your Neighborhood or Town into a Village," 2006 Beacon Hill Village, available at www.beaconhillvillage.org.
8. Kemper, Komisar, and Alecxih, "Long-Term Care Over an Uncertain Future."
9. Ibid.
10. Terry Pristin, "Hot Niche in the Rental Market for the Housing Elderly," *The New York Times* (Feb. 15, 2006).
11. National Alliance for Caregiving and AARP, "Caregiving in the U.S" (April 2004). Retrieved from www.caregiving.org/data/04finalreport.pdf.
12. Ibid.
13. Ibid.
14. National Alliance for Caregiving and Zogby International, "Miles Away: The Metlife Study of Long-Distance Caregiving" (July 2004). Retrieved from www.caregiving.org/data/milesaway.pdf.
15. Michael Copeland, "Your Little Piece of Heaven or Hell— Whether Your Investment in a Home Overseas Is Rewarding or an Unbearable Albatross Depends on How Much Advance Work You Do," *Business 2.0 Magazine* (August 1, 2004).

Chapter 7

1. Kaiser Family Foundation and Health Research & Educational Trust, "Employer Health Benefits, 2006 Annual Survey." Retrieved from www.kff.org/insurance/7527/upload/7527.pdf.
2. Kaiser Family Foundation and Harvard School of Public Health, "Healthcare Costs Survey," *USA Today* (August 2005).
3. Ibid.
4. Himmelstein et al. "Illness and Injury as Contributors to Bankruptcy," Health Affairs, W5-63-73 (February 2, 2005).

5. Carmen DeNavas-Walt, Bernadette D. Proctor, and Cheryl Hill Lee, "Income, Poverty and Health Insurance Coverage in the United States: 2005," U.S. Census Bureau, (August 2006). Retrieved from www.census.gov/prod/2006pubs/p60-231.pdf.

6. Kaiser Family Foundation and Health Research & Educational Trust, "Employer Health Benefits, 2006 Summary of Findings," p. 2.

7. "Squeezed: Why Rising Exposure to Healthcare Costs Threatens the Health and Financial Well-Being of American Families," *The Commonwealth Fund* (September 2006), Retrieved from www.cmwf.org/usr_doc/Collins_squeezedrisinghltcarecosts_953.pdf.

8. U.S. Department of Labor, "Consumer Expenditures in 2005 (February 2007). U.S. Department of Labor Statistics, Report 998.

9. Kaiser Family Foundation and Health Research & Educational Trust, "Employer Health Benefits, 2006 Annual Survey."

10. "Will Health Benefit Costs Eclipse Profits?" *The McKinsey Quarterly Focus Newsletter* (September 2004).

11. Kaiser Family Foundation and Hewitt Associates, "Prospects for Retiree Health Benefits as Medicare Drug Coverage Begins. Findings from the Kaiser/Hewitt 2005 Survey on Retiree Health Benefits," December 7, 2005. Kaiser Family Foundation and Health Research & Educational Trust, "Employer Health Benefits, 2006 Annual Survey."

12. H&R Block, "Tax Tips, Medical Expenses," Retrieved from www.hrblock.com/taxes/tax_tips/deductions_credits/medical_expenses.html.

13. Dennis Cauchon, "Who Will Take Care of an Older Population?" *USA Today* (October 24, 2005).

14. Laurence Kotlikoff and Christian Hagist, "Who's Going Broke?" NBER, Working Paper 11833 (December 2005).

15. Kaiser Family Foundation and Health Research & Educational Trust, "Employer Health Benefits, 2006 Annual Survey."

16. "Health Savings Accounts and Other Tax-Favored Health Plans," IRS Publication 969. Retrieved from www.irs.gov/pub/irs-pdf/p969.pdf.

17. Jack Hadley and John Holahan, "The Cost of Care for the Uninsured: What Do We Spend, Who Pays and What Would Full Coverage Add to Medical Spending? 2004 Issue Update"

Kaiser Commission on Medicaid and the Uninsured (May 10, 2004). Retrieved from www.kff.org/uninsured/upload/ The-Cost-of-Care-for-the-Uninsured-What-Do-We-Spend-Who-Pays-and-What-Would-Full-Coverage-Add-to-Medical-Spending.pdf.

18. Jack Hadley, "Sicker and Poorer—The Consequences of Being Uninsured: A Review of the Research on the Relationship between Health Insurance, Medical Care Use, Health, Work and Income," *Medical Care Research and Review*, vol. 60, no. 2 (Supplement to June 2003).

19. Kemper, Komisar, and Alecxih, "Long-Term Care over an Uncertain Future."

20. "Be Prepared, Government Funding for Nursing Homes May Be Cut," *Wall Street Journal* (September 7, 2005).

21. "The Metlife Market Survey of Nursing Home and Home Care Costs," Metlife, September 2006. Retrieved from www.metlife.com/ WPSAssets/18756958281159455975V1F2006NHHCMarketSurvey. pdf.

22. Numbers from State Farm Long-Term Care Insurance Quote Calculator. www.statefarm.com/apps/hrq/ltcV2/stateSelect_ 01.asp.

23. Stokes Lawrence, "Insight on Estate Planning" (April-May 2007). Retrieved from www.stokeslaw.com/practice/insight_april07. pdf.

24. Kemper, Komisar, and Alecxih, "Long-Term Care over an Uncertain Future."

25. "2004 Disability Status Reports, U.S.," October 2005, Cornell University, Employment and Disability Institute. Kemper, Komisar, and Alecxih, "Long-Term Care over an Uncertain Future."

26. U.S Census Bureau, "Survey of Income and Program Participation" (June-September 2002).

27. "2004 Disability Status Reports, U.S."

28. Insurance Information Institute, www.iii.org/media/facts/ statsbyissue/disability/, citing "2004 Disability Rate Study & Risk Management Survey," JHA.

29. American Academy of Anti-Aging Medicine, "Virtual Medical Checkups on the Rise" (March 21, 2006). Retrieved from www.worldhealth.net/p/virtual-medical-checkups-on-the-rise-2006-03-21.html.

30. "Is the Cost of Healthcare Worth It?" MSNBC, citing *Harvard/ Yale New England Journal of Medicine* (August 30, 2006). www. msnbc.msn.com/id/14588793/

31. Carrie Coolidge, "Die or Your Money Back," *Forbes* (April 24, 2006.) Retrieved from http://members.forbes.com/ forbes/2006/0424/072.html.

32. J.J. MacNab, "Viatical Settlements: Myths and Misconceptions," Planned Giving Design Center (May 2, 2003). Retrieved from www.pgdc.com/usa/item/?itemID=60553, www.longtermcare. gov/LTC/Main_Site/Paying_LTC/Private_Programs/ Other_Insurance/index.aspx.

33. Marilyn Gardner, "How to Beat the Midas Curse," *Christian Science Monitor,* Work & Money, citing Rodney Zeeb (March 13, 2006).

34. John J. Havens and Paul G. Schervish, "Why the $41 Trillion Wealth Transfer Estimate Is Still Valid: A Review of Challenges and Questions," Boston College Social Welfare Research Institute (January 6, 2003). Retrieved from www.bc.edu/research/ swri/meta-elements/pdf/41trillionreview.pdf.

35. John Gist and Carlos Figueiredo, "In Their Dreams: What Will Boomers Inherit?" AARP. www.aarp.org/research/reference/ boomers/dd139_inherit.html.

Index